The Facebook Formula:
How Business Owners
Find Big Profits

Kevin

To your Success

The Facebook Formula: How Business Owners Find Big Profits

A Simple Guide to Better Results

BRIAN HAHN

EXPERT PRESS

The Facebook Formula: How Business Owners Find Big Profits
A Simple Guide to Better Results

ISBN-13: 978-1-946203-60-1

Go Social Experts
www.gosocialexperts.com

.

www.ExpertPress.net

Contents

Chapter One

Who Am I to Give Advice?

MY PARENTS PURCHASED a grocery store in 1978 and it quickly became a family affair with all of us pitching in to make it a local success.

I was 14 when they bought it. And I remember thinking I would love to be able to buy a store when I was older. I loved working with the people and helping them in the store.

But as time went on, it got harder and harder to compete. Ours was a smaller store compared to the large multi-store competitors in our area. Their advertising budgets were much larger than ours and over the years competing became very difficult.

To make matters worse, after 28 years in business, the state built a highway that moved people away from our store, not toward it.

By this time I had taken over the store from my folks and I was trying to figure out what would bring people back to the store.

Local newspaper ads and flyers weren't attracting the customers like they had previously. We were getting some results from the emails we sent out, but it wasn't enough.

And I thought—could social media be the answer?

Facebook was really building momentum at that time and I was curious if Facebook ads and online marketing would drive customers back to our store.

Whenever we did TV, radio, or newspaper ads, one of their respective sales reps would ask a few questions and design a campaign for us that matched our goals and budget. Even better, they'd implement it for us. It wasn't an awful lot of work on our part.

So I assumed, wrongly, that the same was true for Facebook ads and online marketing. But the problem was, I couldn't find anyone who could help!

I searched the internet, called the chamber of commerce, and asked everyone I knew if there was someone in the area that helped businesses with Facebook marketing. I found no one.

So the only option I had was to learn how to use Facebook myself. Fortunately, I enjoyed computers and exploring social media, so learning Facebook and online marketing was a fun adventure with a practical purpose.

I did have to do most of the work after I got my regular work done in the evening, but I was excited to do it. I found an inexpensive course to buy and implemented what was taught. I started getting results.

A few months later I was at a conference and a speaker there talked about using Facebook. At the end of his talk he offered a training program to help with Facebook marketing. I bought it, did everything that was taught, and had even more success for the store.

The challenge was that everything was changing on Facebook so fast that by the time the program was done and I had implemented it, everything had changed, so I began working my own strategies into the programs to make them work. By the time I was finished I had my own system that worked.

Proof of concept

During this time, my sister and I decided to use the Facebook methods we'd had success with for the grocery store and see if it worked in another business of ours.

What do you know, the same tactics worked in this industry—in fact, even better!

My sister and I own five Dairy Queen Restaurants and we tested Facebook in these. After all, if it didn't work, I was the one out the money.

However, it did work. I didn't lose any money. Over the next five years our Dairy Queens increased in sales more than the Dairy Queen System as a whole; in fact it has been substantially more than the average Dairy Queen.

Our sales increases drew the attention of some of the bigwigs at International Dairy Queen. They sent a team of people to our stores to see what we were doing, as our sales were increasing more than any other stores, unless the others had remodeled.

Crossroads

After a few years of working with Facebook for our businesses, I came to a crossroads. My passion wasn't in the grocery business. It was in social media marketing. And I'd developed a system that worked consistently when followed.

It was time to move on.

It was an emotional decision, but I decided it was time to leave the family grocery business behind and to jump into social media and online marketing, especially Facebook Ads, full time.

It was scary, but very rewarding. And as it turns out, very successful.

Since leaving the grocery store and starting Go Social Experts, I've been able to help clients really grow their businesses . . . and profits. The system I've developed has worked for my clients with quick service restaurants, legal practices, dental offices, spas, magazine publishers, and artists.

And it's worked for a variety of really niche markets—for example people who want to learn about horse cutting (it really is a thing!) or take piano lessons online or move everything they own into an RV and travel the country full time.

As I've worked with clients and students all over the country, I've had a chance to see from the inside what creates a successful online marketing strategy and what blocks can stop the success dead in its tracks.

But, you ask, does online marketing actually work?

Can I be painfully honest with you for a moment? Yes, online marketing does work. Yes, many people are getting great (profitable) results from Facebook and other online marketing efforts.

No, you don't have to use it. I know that last line is strange to hear from me. There are many businesses in the world not using Facebook and surviving. Some are even growing.

How do you decide if you are one of those who should use Facebook? Well, the answer depends on what you're trying to accomplish and more importantly, what your goals are.

What are you trying to achieve and why do you want to achieve it? That is the question we need to answer on every level as we're designing our business's plans.

Until you know your goals and where you are trying to go, you can't decide if you should use Facebook or not, if you should use any online marketing or not, or if you should rely solely on referrals and repeat business or not.

As one of my mentors has drilled into my head over time (actually many years, sometimes I'm a slow learner), what are you trying to do and why is it important to you? I can't give you an opinion of what is good or bad or right or wrong as you create your plansuntil you tell me what you're trying to accomplish.

Believe it or not, setting your goals and then actually using your goals as a guide to deciding what to do is one of the basic points that most of us miss.

We set goals—we might even write them down—and then we put them away somewhere and go out and do what we think is best.

After a few weeks, the list is a distant memory. We may not even be able to find it. We go out and chase after the newest shiny object we hear about.

After all, everyone else is doing the same thing and look at the results that "they" are getting. I'm at least as smart as they are so I should be able to do that or better. Right?

Setting your goals and then using them to decide what you should be working on will bring you to your goals faster.

If your goal is to grow and expand your business—and you want to reach new people and maintain a relationship with your existing customers in a low-cost manner—Facebook can be great.

It takes some effort to develop a plan that works, but it can bring huge rewards.

Knowing that you're moving towards your goals and that your life will be better when you achieve those goals gives you fuel for the fire as you're working through anything that gets in your way.

In the following chapters I'm going to reveal to you what it takes to succeed with Facebook and online marketing. Some of it will be obvious; other points may have been hidden. But let's start with the basic question. Of all the social media marketing opportunities, why Facebook?

What's so special about Facebook?

This is a question I'm asked regularly.

After all people tell me there are many other ways to advertise online like:

- Twitter
- LinkedIn
- Pinterest
- Snapchat
- YouTube
- Google AdWords
- Instagram
- WhatsApp
- . . . and more every day

These are the obvious competitors to Facebook, but more and more are being developed all the time. There are too many to list.

First let me define what I mean when I say Facebook. It's a huge platform and it includes more than just the familiar Facebook newsfeed that most people know.

The Facebook ads platform includes:

- Facebook Newsfeed
- Facebook Stories
- Facebook Messenger
- Instagram
- Instagram Stories

- WhatsApp
- The Audience Network—Via its Audience Network, Facebook can display ads in apps and websites beyond the Facebook platform.

As you can see the Facebook newsfeed is only a small part of the Facebook platform.

What makes this powerful is the number of people who use one or more of these apps every day.

How many people?

For starters, more than 2,000,000,000 people use Facebook every month. More than 1,000,000,000 people use Instagram every month. That's a total of over 3,000,000,000 people and that number is growing at a pace of 500,000 new users every day.

These numbers are stunning. Now add to them the fact that the average user spends 20 minutes a day on Facebook. That should give you an idea of why Facebook. But there's more.

Powerful targeting

Combine the number of users with the data Facebook has on all of us and you get a powerful one-two punch. Facebook knows what you do on all the platforms they own, and they also know what you do on many of the websites you visit. There are few if any secrets from Facebook online.

Now that may scare you. But if you're a marketer it may excite you.

After all, putting your best ad in front of someone who doesn't care won't get the response you want.

What does work is matching the perfect message to the perfect person, and Facebook does this better than any other platform.

You can also upload your customer list or your prospect list and if you have more than 100 of them you can target them with Facebook ads too.

Results

All of this lets Facebook deliver results to its advertisers.

Facebook wants you to be successful with your ads. It's their goal for you to profit from your investment. That way you will continue to advertise, and you might even increase the amount of money you spend with them.

Audiences on Facebook and Instagram have been conditioned to buy. Facebook makes it easy for readers to click on posts and go where you want them to, and many do regularly.

It's not uncommon for us to see a return on ad spend of two, three, four, five times or more for every dollar spent. And if you factor in the growth of your audience it can exceed these numbers.

Ease of use

This may be hard for many of you to believe, but it is possible to create your own ads and target the people you want yourself.

Yes, you do need to have some technical skills, and to get results you need to understand what moves people from "I've never heard of you" to "Here's my credit card, please take my money." Once you've developed these skills you can do it yourself.

Think of it, you have access to over three billion people and you can do it all yourself.

Cost

I know Facebook ads are more expensive than they were in the past, but where else can you spend $1 a day and reach hundreds of people every day?

Now that's not free, but if you can't afford to spend $1 a day on your business you might want to look into what your business is and you might want to consider making changes.

And if you want to scale up and reach millions to tens of millions of people you can do so on the same platform.

Last thoughts

The Facebook ads platform is much more than "just" Facebook. It includes Facebook Messenger, Instagram and WhatsApp along with Facebook. From now on when you hear Facebook broaden the platforms you're thinking of.

There are massive audiences of people checking Facebook every day looking for what you're selling. You can reach them on one platform, and you can do it affordably.

So now that we've established the *why* of Facebook marketing, let's turn our attention to the *how*. (If you're impatient, you can see an overview of an entire Facebook and Online Marketing System in a Masterclass I've created. Go to www.gosocialexperts.com/masterclass to access the course.)

Chapter Two

Online Marketing is Still Marketing
(and yes, you need to actively market your social media)

I'M WILLING TO BET that when you think of using Facebook and online marketing for your business you are thinking of it as a strategy.

I mean . . . that's what all of us marketing experts beat into everyone's heads, *right?*

You have to be cunning and smart. You have to anticipate your customer's needs and be two steps ahead of them so you can get the sale.

But I'm wondering if thinking of Facebook and online marketing as a strategy isn't what creates so many challenges for businesses. We sometimes spend days trying to develop new strategies for online marketing, when we might not need to.

One of my marketing mentors said something like this at an event, and it's been on my mind ever since.

At first, I thought, of course Facebook is a strategy! But after a bit of consideration, I've changed my opinion.

Facebook and the internet are media. Why do I say that? Facebook is a great tool to use to reach your audience wherever they are. However, radio, TV, and newspapers all do that too.

But there are significant differences between Facebook and these traditional media. For example, your audience can respond to your ads and posts on Facebook and they can easily share your information with their friends and family.

This makes Facebook more than a broadcast medium. Facebook

is a tool that gives a business a chance to have conversations with its customers.

Think about the power of that. Not only can you get your message out, you can also see in real time how your audience responds.

But really, why does it matter if Facebook is a medium or a strategy?

When you look at Facebook as a strategy you must figure out how you're going to use it and develop a plan that you can implement. There's a lot of brainpower that has to go into that.

When you look at Facebook as a medium you can look at what you've done in other media (either online or offline) that people responded to and then apply that to Facebook.

You do need to make adaptations for the differences between Facebook and traditional media, but the overall strategy is the same. This gives you a great place to start and can be much less overwhelming for a new or expanding Facebook and online marketer.

Facebook is a powerful medium that gives you the chance to find your ideal audience and reach them wherever they are on the device they happen to be using. It doesn't matter if they're waiting for their kids at the bus stop or standing in line at the grocery store; if they have a device in their hand (and who doesn't nowadays?), you can talk to them.

You don't have to hope they pick up the newspaper or have time to sit down at home and watch television.

Along with being able to reach people wherever they are, you can also show them videos, audio, pictures, or just plain old text all on one platform. You can't do that on any of the traditional media. Taking a strategy you know works and adapting it to Facebook can give you fast results.

Organic Facebook Marketing: A Quick Start Guide

A while back a friend who owns a business asked me if we could meet for lunch. He had some questions about using Facebook to promote his business and wanted more information.

I accepted and looked forward to meeting with him. We hadn't talked for some time and it was a great excuse to connect.

After we talked a bit he asked me what I would do if I were just getting started with

Facebook and online marketing and I only had a small budget.

I've had other people ask me this too, so I thought that you might find what I told him interesting. Here is what I would do if I had a small business and wanted to use Facebook to promote it.

First, let me clarify. There are two separate uses of Facebook. One is organic, which is the unpaid exposure you get when you post, comment, or share. The other is the paid ads side of Facebook. With paid ads, you can reach out to millions of people even if you have no followers.

Let's start with organic reach. The better you get at organic strategies and implementation, the better your ads will do.

Facebook loves to see meaningful interaction with all the information you post—your organic posts as well as your ads. The more meaningful interaction your page has, the more people you'll reach and the cheaper your ads will be.

Step One: Know what you want to achieve.

- Do you want to get new customers?
- Do you want your existing customers to buy more from you?
- Do you want your existing customers to come back more often and stay connected to you longer?

All of these are possible, just not at the same time.

Step Two: Create a sales-oriented Facebook page.

This means you've designed your page in such a way that people are encouraged to find you from your Facebook page.

A sales-oriented Facebook page includes a great cover photo with a call to action, a profile picture that your audience recognizes, an "About" area filled out completely, and great videos and pictures that engage your audience.

To download a checklist that you can use to audit your page go to www.gosocialexperts.com/checklist

Step Three: Post consistently.

The people who have "liked" your page get used to seeing your posts in their newsfeeds, but if you don't post or you stop posting all your momentum stops.

It's like the exercise machine you bought two years ago that you use to hang clothes on now. You've taken action, but you're not seeing the results you expected.

Once you put posting on Facebook into your routine you can do it fairly easily, but if you stop posting, getting started again takes more effort.

I recommend posting a minimum of three times a week to show consistent activity, but I recommend a minimum of once a day for any kind of organic exposure, and multiple times a day if you're serious about growing your presence organically.

Regular posting will ensure that your audience has a better chance of seeing you. As you get more interaction on your Facebook page, Facebook's algorithm will show your posts to more people. Currently, Facebook favors comments and shares over reactions. However, this could change at any time and without notice.

Step Four: Grow your Facebook likes.

Yes, you heard that right.

I put this after posting consistently, because if you get people to come to your page and they're looking around and the last post happened six months ago, do you think they're going to trust you or like your page?

Not likely.

When someone shows up on a Facebook page that doesn't have activity the page feels like a deserted cabin. You know—one that has been sitting empty for months, where there is dust on everything and cobwebs in the corner and weeds growing outside.

When you're growing your likes, make sure they are legitimate likes from people who may be interested in what you offer. You do this by targeting existing customers and people who are interested in products or services that you offer.

Each of these likes have a value far in excess of being a vanity number to look at. And yes, it feels good to go to your Facebook page and see that hundreds or thousands of people "like" you or your page.

The value in legitimate likes is that people have self-identified as potential customers. Many times when we're promoting items using Facebook ads, we target our Facebook fans and they usually respond better for less money than other audiences do.

Also, every like you get is an endorsement to the likers' friends. Yes, you can target friends of your fans and this audience consistently responds well to any ad that you show them.

When this group sees an ad, the name of the friend or friends who like this company are mentioned at the top of the ad. When I see that on an ad, it makes me stop and look at the offer. After all, if my friends like something, there is a good chance that I will too.

Every like you get can bring you 100, 200, or more potential prospects because their friend is telling them that they found what you offer valuable.

Step Five: Start mixing in information about what you're doing in your business.

When you've built an audience of people who are interested in what you do, they want to know what's happening in your business and what's happening in your industry. Some behind-the-scenes posts are always popular.

Talk about:

- Events you're having
- Sales
- New classes
- New products
- How to use your products
- People who have had success
- Testimonials from happy customers

- Charities you support
- Good you do in the community
- Etc.

Once you start looking into how you can use Facebook, more and more ideas will come to you.

The key to being successful with Facebook is to use a mixture of posts with different topics. Some of the posts can be text posts, but you'll want pictures and video on your page too.

The more video you use the faster you'll see results. The video doesn't have to be you talking on camera. It can be shots of your store or place of business, it can be testimonials, or it can be a photo slideshow with you or one of your staff narrating.

There are many options for video. Look for opportunities to create videos and before long you'll be comfortable making them.

The key to succeeding here is to use a proper blend of promotional posts with informational fun posts. You can post promotional posts once a week as long as you have other posts too. If you're posting multiple times a day you'll find you can mix in promotional posts two or three times a week and you'll get a good response.

Step Six: Check your results.

Facebook gives you many tools to see how your posts are doing. On each post, you'll see the reach, reactions, comments, Likes, and shares just to get you started. Scanning this will show you what topics are popular with your audience. Do more of what's working and replace what's not working.

In the Insights tab at the top of your page, you're going to get information about your likes. You'll be able to see where your likes are from, their age, gender, and more.

You'll also be able to see when your fans are on Facebook, which posts have the best reach and engagement, and you can sort your posts so finding which are best is easily done inside Facebook.

There is a plethora (fun word to use) of information about your fans in your Insights tab. Make sure to check it out regularly.

Step Seven: Relax and have fun!

Remember, Facebook and social media are supposed to be fun.

Don't get uptight about every post. If you put one up and it doesn't work as well as you hoped, put up another one later that day; if that works, put up more like it. Remember, Facebook moves fast.

Working on Facebook can become your favorite part of the day. Make sure you have a way to track your results, so that you know the time you spend is being invested in helping your business succeed.

As with any strategy that brings success, it takes some practice. Put in the time to learn what works organically and you'll be on your way to seeing faster results when you start paid advertising.

This should get you going. After a few weeks of using this strategy, and of course, reading this book . . . you'll be all set to start running some PAID Facebook ads!

Case Study: Facebook 101—Getting Started

Can you help me learn how to use Facebook? I was so excited I had to pinch myself when I received this message from one of my clients, Bob and Deb Grinde, from Grinde's Garden Center. You see, they had started to work on Facebook and wanted to do everything themselves. But their efforts were scattered and they hadn't seen any results.

They were getting close to their busy season (they do 90 percent of their business in three months) and they finally came to the conclusion that trying to figure out how to market on Facebook (and keep up with it) was keeping them from providing the great service to their customers that they were known for.

After working with me and getting specific instructions on how to attract their target market, they started posting information that others found interesting and their audience on Facebook grew rapidly. People responded to their content by liking the post, sharing it with their friends, and most importantly—coming to their business more often.

What did they do to make this happen?

- First, they spruced up their Facebook page, organized it and made it look good.
- Next, they committed to posting consistently. They posted a quote related to their product every morning, with bonus posts later in the day. (I helped them streamline and automate this.) This helped them get new customers as well as reactivate customers who hadn't visited their shop for quite a while.
- They systematically posted content with special offers that brought customers to their shop. Their sales increased.
- And finally, they continued to promote posts at key times for their business.

What was the result of these efforts?

"It was our best year ever!" exclaimed Bob in his laid-back style.

To accomplish all of the above easier and faster they used some of the tools we recommend:

- The Facebook Scheduling tool, which is built into Facebook and free to use.

- They chose Stencil, a Chrome plug-in, that provides power-ful tools for editing photos and putting quotes on them easily and effortlessly. This gave them great posts that their audience enjoyed and responded to.

This is what happened to Bob and Deb the first year we worked together. Then they took the winter off and the next spring we worked together again.

So what happens the second and third year you use Facebook to promote your business? People get used to seeing you on Facebook especially in the season that they are thinking about working in their yards. And they come to you for their seeds, plants and hanging baskets.

In fact more and more come every year. Each year that we've helped Bob and Deb promote their business, their business has increased. Each year at the end of the season it's been the 'best year' ever.

They have a local business and their targeting is easy. They are known in the area for their quality products and great service and their business has continued to thrive with Facebook helping keep them in front of their customers.

Chapter Three

How Do You Know That Your Facebook Efforts Are Paying Off?

LET'S FACE IT—getting started with any new skill is tough. And when you're not sure of what you're supposed to do to get results, it's even harder.

Many people ask me about their Facebook pages when we talk. They wonder if what's happening with their page is normal or if it's worth their time. They're finding that the only people who are interacting with their page are people who they know. But isn't Facebook supposed to be about reaching new people?

Well, yes, it is but . . .

When you're getting started with a Facebook page or becoming active again after some time away from Facebook, you're going to find that the only people who are seeing your page are your personal connections—which many times are your family and friends.

This is okay and it's normal.

Facebook shows your organic posts to people it thinks are most likely to want to see them. Which usually seems like a lot less people then we think it should be.

Basically, Facebook is looking for interaction. Are people responding by liking, sharing or commenting on your posts? When they do, Facebook shows them more of your posts and so on.

There are three stages that all Facebook pages go through as they are getting started or if they're restarting after an absence.

When you don't use Facebook regularly, Facebook assumes that you aren't active anymore. That means when you come back you need to prove to Facebook that you're still interesting to your followers.

You will find that you will get traction faster if you had a page in the past. It's like riding a bike. You can go decades without getting on a bike at all but when you do finally climb back on, you'll pick it back up pretty quickly.

Stages of Facebook page growth

Stage One is creating the page and then inviting all your personal Facebook connections to like the page. All you have to do is click a button and Facebook sends them all an invite. Great, right?

This doesn't cost any money, and your connections will get a personal invitation to like your page. This is where having a personal following when you start will help.

If your connections are interested in what you're doing, they will like your page and you're off. The better your relationship with your existing connections, the more of them who will like your page.

The reality is, many of these people will be family and friends. And you may be thinking, so what? They already know about what I do and it doesn't matter to them. However, they have friends and their friends have friends, etc. Like the old adage says, we're only separated by six degrees from everyone on the planet—including your ideal customer.

In **Stage Two**, you'll see people you know of but only at a distance engaging on your page. Your family and friends have shared a post and one of their friends saw it. Or your distant cousin you only see once every year or two saw something you posted and they shared it.

In **Stage Three**, you start seeing people engaging on your page that you don't know. It's a great feeling when you see a like, comment or share from a person you don't know. You're making progress. At first, it doesn't seem like there are many. But as you keep posting and interacting you'll see more and more of them.

How do you keep the growth going?

Simple—Keep posting great information to your audience. As you develop your relationship with them you're going to find your audience growing.

This won't be the only focus of your page, but as you use this audience to test your message and see how they respond, you'll get customers and sales. Basically, you'll be growing a base of people you can reach out to at any time. This group of people can become devoted Facebook fans as well as some of your most loyal customers.

Growing your tribe of people on Facebook shouldn't be your primary goal in using Facebook, but it should be a secondary goal. Over time you'll find that everything you do on Facebook will get better results when you have a larger base to work from.

The good news is that this can all happen organically, without any paid Facebook work. Just understand that it will take time. Every like you get is an endorsement of your page to all the liker's friends. It is a very powerful word-of-mouth tool.

Next steps

Imagine for a moment that it's one year from now and you have a Facebook marketing machine automatically bringing you a steady flow of new customers easily and effortlessly.

This can happen but it will take more than creating a few posts and connecting with others on Facebook.

As I'm sure you've seen, Facebook does limit who your posts are shared with, and unless Facebook deems it worthy you will only reach a small percentage of your audience.

While this organic approach doesn't cost as much cash, it does take your time. And I don't know about you, but I value my time more every year.

Yes, you can and should use Facebook organically, but to speed up your results you must add paid efforts. When you do, you'll find that your organic efforts start to show better results too.

For example, I was just looking at a video that we had promoted for one of our clients. It was a good video that showed my client's business on the Today show. We took that clip and posted it on Facebook.

Now if we stopped there we would have gotten 15,000 to 20,000 views, which is pretty good.

However, as of last night, we had 168,000 total views: 101,493 of them were paid and 66,507 of them were organic.

We would have never reached this level of organic exposure without adding the paid effort, and the earlier organic work we had done having paid off. We already had an audience that is connected to us and growing every day, and campaigns like these help it grow faster.

A Facebook strategy that is effective—that is, profitable—is one which uses all the tools available. You won't reach your full potential if you only use organic or paid marketing alone.

With various strategies, you may want to invest more energy in the organic or paid options, but you'll want to use both throughout your Facebook marketing efforts. Don't limit your success by deciding before you begin that you'll only use organic or paid strategies. Be open to experimenting and expand on what works.

Slow long-lasting success or fast "here today, gone tomorrow" results?

If you want to build a long-term machine that brings you a steady flow of new customers and avoid getting SLAPPED by Facebook algorithm changes—this will be the most important chapter you'll ever read.

Facebook wants people to have fun while on Facebook so they keep coming back. This means Facebook is looking for signs of engagement. Some of these signs are reactions, comments, and shares. Facebook uses these signs to judge if a post or ad is valuable to the readers, and if the signs aren't there Facebook limits the reach of the post or ad.

After all, if people stop coming to Facebook as often they no longer have a viable service. Thus, Facebook works hard to make sure its readers have a good experience.

There are some "experts" out there getting some fantastic results one day and then everything evaporates overnight.

What happened?

They were using a weakness in Facebook's algorithm to get these results. Likely Facebook found the glitch in their system and closed the loophole. And now their whole business stops until they find another solution—or their business goes away altogether.

This is known as a Black Hat Tactic.

These tactics provide no value to the consumer, or to Facebook, and are only used to sell their product. As soon as Facebook finds this out they change the rules. The tactic won't work, and the account may be banned. There are organic black hat tactics as well as black hat tactics for paid ads but both end with the same result.

Some examples of Black Hat Tactics are:

- Pictures that hint at something other than what they really are.
- Headlines that hint one thing and deliver another when you click on the post.
- Buying likes for your page. (Yes, you can buy them.)

These practices are all against Facebook's Terms of Service.

The challenge with using these tactics is that they only work short term. I don't know about you, but I'm building a business for the long term. I have no interest in tactics that only work for a few weeks or months.

Next on our list is Gray Hat Tactics. These are a tough call. They aren't really against Facebook terms of service, but Facebook doesn't really like them either. And once Facebook decides they don't like something, they usually change it. What is considered a gray hat tactic one day can change to a white or black hat tactic on another day with just a slight change of Facebook's policy.

One example of this is Facebook contests. In the past, you had to use an app to run a contest, so if you ran a contest in your newsfeed (asking people to answer a trivia question, for example) you were in violation of Facebook terms. Facebook has now changed this so you can run contests in your newsfeed, but they may change their mind anytime and this will be against the rules again.

On to White Hat Tactics

These are my favorites. These tactics work all the time. Facebook changes come and your posts keep getting better and better results.

Facebook is really looking for businesses that are willing to interact and give to their readers. Once Facebook knows that you do that they reward you with traffic. Lots of traffic.

And interacting and giving to your readers is becoming important even if you're running ads.

The ways you do this is to make sure that your followers want to see your posts. You do this by posting information they want to see. This can be pictures, videos, links to other articles, or even text posts. What's important is that your audience interacts with what you post.

To make this happen you need to know what your audience wants and you need to improve the quality of your posts. Do they want funny pictures and posts, great information about how to do something, inspirational posts, or information about what you're doing and why you're doing it?

One thing to keep in mind when you're interacting on Facebook is that people are more interested in what you're doing and experiencing than in what you can teach them. You need to demonstrate your expertise, and it's possible to provide examples with much less time devoted to this demonstration and more devoted to creating the relationship.

Another consideration is how consistent you are in using Facebook. Do you post regularly or are there large gaps in your posting schedule? The more consistent you are, the better Facebook likes it.

Facebook really likes it when you talk about trending topics and join in the conversation with your fans about what is happening. How can you tie what you do into what is happening on Facebook and in the world?

As you get better at creating engagement with your customers you'll find more and more people seeing your posts no matter what Facebook does with their algorithm.

Take some time developing your White Hat Facebook strategy and then implement it. As you put it into place you'll be developing an asset you'll have for years to come.

When you are running paid ads, the better you are at creating posts that your audience is interested in, the cheaper it will be to get clicks on your ads. Which in turn means the faster you'll sell your products and services.

Chapter Four

Is There a Marketing Ninja Move to Turbocharge Your Facebook Marketing?

WE ALL WANT the cool trick that can move our Facebook marketing from *It's going okay . . .* to *Oh my gosh, I can't handle the business.*

People come to me regularly and want to know what kind of ninja Facebook trick will make their Facebook marketing work.

There are many essentials to setting up the basics of a Facebook campaign but the most important item needed isn't a ninja Facebook trick.

What is it, you ask? It's getting your message right.

We've had this happen to us here at Go Social Experts. When we are offering a new product, we're excited about what we developed and how much it can do for our clients and students.

We put it into a test and get poor results. We adjust it and try again—and again.

Over the past few months we've been targeting grocery store owners with an offer to create and manage their Facebook campaigns for them.

When we started we thought our audience wanted one thing, and that they would respond to a particular message. Well, it turns out that they didn't. We had to go back to the drawing board to find out what they would respond to. After some adjustments we started to see results from our marketing efforts to the grocers.

Finding out what your audience wants to know about and how they respond is all part of creating a great campaign. We put ourselves in our customer's shoes and ask: *If I could just_____?*

One thing to keep in mind is that your customer doesn't care about your services or products. What they want to know is what results they are going to get. You are in the way of their having everything they want. You are a roadblock.

Your message needs to convey what they can have and how their life is going to be better with your product. How is your customer's life going to be better by buying from you?

- Are they going to have more money?
- Will they have less stress?
- Are they going to have more status than they do now?
- How is their life going to be easier?

Now the real challenge is how to uncover this information. You may think you know, but if you aren't getting a response you are missing something.

So what happens if you're out of ideas and you still haven't gotten the results you wanted? Ask your audience. This can be an email or a question on social media.

Develop five or six questions that will give you the information you need to develop your message. Questions like:

- What causes you the most frustration when _____?
- What keeps you up late at night_____?
- If you could have anything you wanted about _____ what would it be?
- In your wildest dreams you would ask for _____.

After you get this feedback you can make another try at creating your message. Once you have a message that your audience responds to, then you can expand your advertising efforts and start getting results. Until you get your message dialed in, you'll spend your time and money trying to make the different techniques work and not see the results you want.

This is what I tell people: No matter how good my skills are at setting up the technology for your Facebook campaign, if you don't have the right message we're not going to get the best results possible.

Take the time to get your message right and all your marketing will be easier.

The expert tip I disagree with

What you're about to read goes against what you've probably heard from other experts. They've told you time and time again not to do this. But I just can't keep quiet—this is the expert tip I disagree with *a lot.*

The whole point of social media is it gets your message out there to your audience—but what if they don't care about what you have to say? What if they don't want to hear your message? In this chapter, I'm going to share with you a four-step system for testing your messages. It's one that you can set up in minutes and have results in less than two days—so that you know if your message is a winner.

Find out if your message is going to work

It doesn't matter if you are using paid ads or organic posts. You have time invested in both. And if you're running ads, you're spending cold hard cash. You want the most compelling message.

When you are paying money to get people to do what you want, you want to make sure you're getting the best possible results before investing too much.

When you're running ads, one of the most important pieces is the message you're promoting. Once you have your message down and you know your audience responds to it, you are well on your way to having a successful campaign.

Facebook engagement is a good thing

Once your audience gets used to seeing you in their newsfeed, and they like what they are seeing, you're going to have people commenting and sharing your posts. And in the end, it doesn't matter if they are paid or organic posts because it lets you reach more people without spending money.

Many times our ads are shared by our audience. It happens regularly when you have a strong relationship with them.

Facebook likes to see your audience engaging with your content. When they do, it tells Facebook that people want to see your post so they show it to more people organically, even if ittarted as an ad.

Step One: Create a saved audience

The first step of the process of testing your message is to set up a saved audience in the Ads Manager. This will enable you to choose with more precision who sees your ad. You're looking to test your message to your ideal audience, not just any audience that Facebook chooses.

Go to the Audience tab in Ads Manager and create a saved audience. This ensures that you're talking to the same people multiple times. After all, familiarity is what makes people comfortable with you and your business.

Step Two: Create a page post

Next step is to put the post you want to use on your page. Yes, just a regular post. It's best if you use a picture or two or a video in the post, but just create a post for the message you want to test.

Once that's done you click the "boost post" button on the bottom left of the post. YES, the very button that I and most other Facebook experts have been telling you not to ever use. You see, Facebook has made changes to how this button works and now you have more control over who sees your ad with this button.

Step Three: Select your audience

While boosting the post you're going to get the chance to select the targeting. You can boost it to an audience you create, or fans and friends of fans, or you can choose a previously saved audience, like the one we created in step one.

IMPORTANT: Select the saved audience you created earlier as the targeting option. The only time to use your friends and fans is if you have carefully built your fan base organically and you know they are interested in your products and services. In this case you may want to test how your fans and their friends respond.

Step Four: Set your budget

The budget you want for this is $20, and you want to spend it over two days. This will show your post to about 1000 people and you will have data that tells you how they responded.

How well did you do?

Facebook gives every ad a rating. In the past they gave a relevance score which showed you how well your audience responded to your message on a scale of 1 to 10.

Currently Facebook has broken this number down into three more granular metrics. The new metrics are quality ranking, engagement rate ranking and conversion rate ranking. The quality ranking metric will measure an ad's perceived quality compared to other ads competing for the same target market.

The engagement rate metric will show an ad's expected engagement rate compared to ads competing for the same audience.

The conversion rate ranking shows an ad's expected conversion rates when compared to other ads with the same optimization goals and audience.

Having these three rankings to work with will let you see how your ad is doing and what needs to be adjusted if you're not getting the results you want.

Now remember the results you really want is your end goal, not just good Facebook numbers. Use these metrics as a guide only if you're looking for ways to improve your results.

Run with the winners

You will find that you'll have more mediocre or poor posts than winners, especially at first. The idea is to find the winners quickly and cheaply and run with those. When you have a winner, put money and time behind it and watch your results come in.

Once you have done this one time, you're going to be able to use it over and over again to test each message or ad before you spend a significant amount of time on it.

Case Study: Will Facebook work for your retail store?

I want to tell you about Mike. His story will inspire you.

Mike has a retail store in the Tacoma, Washington area that sells motorcycle gear to riders. They are the premier destination for motorcycle gear and accessories, a true riders' shopping experience in the Northwest and online.

Mike is progressive in his marketing. He was one of the first people into Facebook marketing and he's put this experience to good use.

Here is what Mike does.

He works hard at creating different audiences to talk to. He has over 32,000 likes on his Facebook page. This gives him an audience who like to hear from him and they do respond well to fun posts as well as his ads. It's amazing seeing the likes, comments, and shares he gets even on an ad.

Next, he works to add people from his Facebook likes to his email list. This gives him another way to connect; the ones who are willing to share their contact information are more engaged with his store and are customers who spend more money with him. If they don't spend as much at first, they become higher spending customers as they remain on his email list longer.

To grow his email list, he offers people not on his mailing list a coupon for a discount in his store. They go to a web page to sign up and then the coupon is emailed to them. The new subscriber currently has 14 days to use the coupon.

Mike tracks how many coupons come in and most months the amount spent from this one strategy more than covers the cost of all his Facebook campaigns.

Next, Mike targets these audiences when he has events at the store. An event can be reps from manufacturers coming in, coffee and donuts on Saturday mornings, rides starting or ending at the stores, new products coming in, sales reps from different manufacturers on hand or special sales.

Having the list of people to talk to amps up the success he has with all of these events, and you notice that many of them don't involve price discounts.

However, Mike doesn't stop with this work. He wants more sales and knows there are many other tools that he can use.

He finds new people who may not know about his store by advertising great articles that his ideal customers are interested in. One of his most popular is The Top 20 Must-See Motorcycle Rides in the U.S.

People who go to this post are most likely to be motorcycle riders, so using the Facebook pixel (more about that in Chapter Nine) we show ads for his stores to people who go to this article. We do limit the ads to people living in the area of his stores. This gives us a steady stream of new customers.

One last strategy that we've just started using for him is separating out what items people are looking at on his website and sending them an offer for one of those items. If someone is looking at helmets we have an offer for helmets; if men's jackets they get an offer for men's jackets; if ladies boots they get an offer for ladies boots.

We are able to offer this only to people who haven't bought yet, so if someone buys an item they won't see future offers for the same item.

All in all, this adds up to a powerful Facebook marketing system. Mike has worked on it for years and he gets great results.

What kind of results? Well, Mike is a good businessman and measures everything he can. Though not everything can be measured, month after month he sees a positive return on investment (ROI) on what he spends on Facebook for marketing.

Some months he only doubles his money. Other months, he gets a return of four or five times his spending, all depending on what events he has going on, and sometimes the time of year.

Let's face it, when it is marginally above freezing it's not as much fun to ride a motorcycle. While some do, many don't or at least not as often.

With some planning and execution, you can set up a system like this for your retail store. It isn't complicated once it's set up and it's not expensive to implement.

Chapter Five

Are You Building a Business or Looking for a One-Hit Wonder?

IMAGINE FOR A MINUTE that it's five years from now and you have a successful business. What does it look like? How did you get here?

Has your business been a string of one-hit promotions that you put together one after another, or has it been a process of building up a successful system that brings you a steady flow of new customers and then nurtures them until they become devoted followers?

I reviewed the clients I've served over the past few years and examined the ones we've led to the greatest success. Our most successful campaigns were those that had one of two different characteristics.

The first type of successful campaign was for clients who had great products and offers. They put together killer offers, we got the targeting right, and together we sold these products.

The other successful group was made up of clients who had good products, but who had to work a little harder. These clients didn't stop with the first offer. They developed plans to reach those people who had bought even a single item from them, nurtured the relationships, and sold more products to them. They grew businesses out of those initial sales.

First, I need to explain what I mean by one-hit wonders. In the music business, this term refers to an artist who has a single huge hit and then never has one again. Many times, their one hit comes early in their career, and they don't repeat it. These are songs like Johnny Lee's "Lookin' for Love," or Devo's "Whip It" from the 1980s. They were both huge songs, but the acts didn't repeat with other hits after these. In fact many of you will have to Google them to find out who sang the songs.

In terms of physical products, one-hit wonders are items like pet rocks, Cabbage Patch Kids, and the Rubik's Cube. They take off, sell millions, and then disappear.

One-hit wonders are great. They generate cash—sometimes a great deal of it. You find an item you can sell, and then you find people who you think will like it and offer it and it takes off. This generates a great cash flow, and many times businesses are founded upon such products. If you're just getting started, you need to have a success right away to keep your business going. You don't have time to develop it any further, at least not at first. You're busy just keeping up with the orders going out the door.

All you have to set up is a page that explains your product and a checkout page to collect money and collect the shipping information. Then your products are out the door and gone and the money is in your checkbook!

You set up a Facebook ad and bring people to your page. They buy and *voilà!* You have an online business. It's good times.

And by the way, when I get to create ads for a "hot" product, it is fun. I get to look at how much we can sell and the cost per sale. The numbers are large and the numbers keep getting better and bigger and they're fun to look at. It's exhilarating!

If you don't develop a way to follow up on this hit or discover how to sell another product or service, this is it. When you run out of steam and the fad passes, there is nothing left to sell. You didn't build anything to help you grow bigger. The challenge is to move on to something else.

I've found that with a little thought, effort, and work while you are in the middle of the chaos of your first success, you can put in place systems that help you create a lasting business.

Long-term success

Another way you can approach Facebook marketing is as an entire system. You use it to sell your products and grow your audience at the same time.

Yes, selling products is necessary, but selling a product the first time is only the beginning. The most successful businesses don't care whether they make a profit the first time they sell an item. What they really want is the customer. They want a person willing to pay them money for what they're selling over and over again.

This may sound silly—but many times people say they want something and want to buy it, but when it comes time to pay, they aren't willing to actually put up the money. The hardest thing is getting the first sale from a customer and it doesn't matter how much the first sale is.

Once you get the first sale, don't stop there.

A Facebook system that's designed to build your business will be built to capture the contact information of not just your customers, but everyone you encounter. This will be supplemented with email and possibly direct mail.

This system is far more than just Facebook ads. It is online marketing and it has many moving parts and different components. Pieces like landing pages, opt-in pages, thank you pages, and email autoresponders.

A system that's designed to grow your business won't be starved for investment. If you are creating sales, you will want to have the best tools you can get.

After all the best craftsmen and the most successful businesses have the tools they need to get the job done. The tools may or may not be the latest version, but they do the job and get the results you're looking for.

Many times, I see people starving their business of necessary tools because they don't want to spend the monthly fees the services would cost. Yes, I like free and low-cost tools, but only if they don't slow down my business's growth. If it takes investing money to grow, invest it. Once you have momentum, don't slow down. Keep it going.

One of the keys to an effective Facebook marketing machine is constantly building your audiences. You will be gathering email addresses, Facebook Likes, and website custom audiences from people who interact with you on Facebook and who go to your website.

As you gather these audiences and interact with them, you develop a positive relationship. This involves educating them as well as entertaining them. You want everyone to know that you can help them succeed and that you are the type of person with whom they want to do business.

These lists of people and your relationship with them are the most valuable assets you have.

As your audiences grow, you have more people who are familiar with you, and as long as they had a positive experience with your company they will buy from you again and again.

Now you have your base of first-time customers growing. What's next?

Sell them something else. Hopefully, you have another product or service to offer or you can offer more of the first product they purchased.

The key is to work with this audience. The more familiar people are with your products and services, the more likely they are to buy from you when they need what you sell.

As you add new people to these lists through selling a hot product or through other marketing, your audience expands and you will be consistently growing your business.

Facebook can help make all of this happen at a price you can afford. While you are testing, you can spend as little as five dollars a day. Once you know your system is working you can increase the amount your spending and increase the reach of your ads.

There are multiple targeting options when you are looking for new customers, and Facebook is very good at identifying these people for you.

The exciting part of this is that Facebook is growing. As big as the platform already is, there are new people all over the world connecting on Facebook. What's even more exciting is that many of them log on to Facebook every day and spend time on it regularly. Even long-time Facebook users continue to spend a growing portion of their online time using Facebook.

Keys to fast results:

If you've ever wondered why some businesses can jump on Facebook and grow a large engaged audience with what seems like little effort while you feel like you must struggle for every like—consider this:

- How well known are you to the people you're marketing to?
- If you're a local business, have you been in business in the same town for weeks, months, or years?
- Is your physical location in a place where people drive by it regularly?
- What kind of marketing have you done in the past? Networking, Newspaper, Radio, TV LinkedIn, Twitter?
- How large is your customer base, both past and present?
- How happy is your base with the services you provided?
- What kind of relationship do you have with these people outside of them being your customers?

How you answer these questions will give you a guide to how fast you can expect results. After all, when you have an existing relationship with people it's much faster to move that online or offline and you don't have to start from zero.

If your audience is in a regional or national area some of the same questions should resonate with you as well. For the larger geographic areas, you still are part of a community. When I was in the grocery business, I had connections around the country and we met at trade shows. This is true in most industries.

But what does this have to do with growing a large presence on Facebook?

I often talk about the "temperature" of an audience when I'm talking with clients and we're developing their marketing message to use.

COLD = Brand new audience, no one has heard of you.

WARM = They've heard of you. They may not be ready to buy or know a lot about you, but your name/brand is familiar.

HOT = They know you, they love you, and they're ready to buy.

The more people who know you, the faster and easier you can grow your audience on Facebook and heat them up.

This means that a local business isn't really starting with nothing on Facebook even if they don't have any online presence at all. Those people who have been driving by your business or have been customers or clients for years are willing to follow you on Facebook with little effort on your part. The same is true of regional or national businesses that have been in business for years in their market. These types of businesses often see faster success with Facebook marketing.

Does this mean that if you're new in business or new to a market that you can't use Facebook? No, it doesn't! It just means that it's going to take more effort to get the same results. Not only do you have to get your message dialed in you need to educate your audience about who you are and you must help them get to know like and trust you. This can be done more easily with the right strategy from the start.

Yes, you can do this

Every business that is serious about marketing online should consider implementing a system like this to grow business faster. *Go Social Experts Success System for Facebook* is an inexpensive way to reach out to people who are interested in what you're selling and connect with them while strengthening your relationship.

Imagine what it would mean to your business to have your own success system for Facebook and what you can do with it.

You'll have a steady supply of customers and leads coming to your business—to your physical location, your website, or both if you prefer.

This gives you the opportunity to grow your business to whatever size you want. You are in charge of your success rather than relying on the whims of fate or anyone else's favors. You have the power to create the change in your business.

Now the challenge is to get started if you haven't yet, or if you have, to fine-tune your system, test and adjust.

If you look at all the components and information as one massive project you have to accomplish all at once, you're going to feel overwhelmed.

You're better off breaking it into smaller pieces and conquering each one step at a time. After all, as the old joke goes, how do you eat an elephant?

Well, how do you?

One bite at a time.

The point is to make sure you are making steady progress toward getting your success system built.

When you break down a big project into smaller tasks, it doesn't feel overwhelming and, after a few days of taking steady action, you'll see your project begin to take shape.

The key is to take time every now and then to look back at where you started and see how far you've come.

If you're like me and many others, we keep our eyes focused on where we're going and rarely look back. Even if we've come 600 miles on a 1,000 mile journey, we feel there is still so much to do.

The pitfall with this is it's often easy to feel overwhelmed by what's left to do and not recognize how far you've progressed. This may lead to feeling down about where you're at, and if you're not careful, this can stall your progress.

Keep your eye on where you're going but remember to celebrate all the milestones you achieve along the way.

Lessons learned chopping wood

I once spent a week in the Boundary Waters Canoe Area on the U.S.-Canadian border.

This is the type of area where you pack in everything you need, and you pack out anything you have left over. So needless to say, we don't bring in extra tools and the ones we bring in are lightweight.

Plus, no power tools were allowed, so no chainsaws. Hand tools were all that were permitted.

For our group, the main source of cooking was a wood fire. We cooked two meals a day over the fire, so it's safe to say that in seven days we used a fair amount of wood.

It was a group project to collect the wood, cut it and, if needed, split it into smaller pieces. With the tools we had, we could handle wood up to about a 12-inch diameter.

I didn't have much experience splitting wood so I thought I would give it a try. The tool we had to use was a Gerber hatchet, and for the size wood we were using, it was adequate. The trick is to look for a spot on the chunk that is starting to split already and hit it there so it will split in two.

I surveyed a chunk of wood and found what I thought was its weakness right in the middle. I wound up and WHACK—down came the hatchet. The hatchet sank into the wood an inch and stopped. It didn't split. It was just a chunk of wood stuck to a hatchet.

As one of the older, more experienced members watched me try and hammer the hatchet through the center of the chunk, he mentioned that it might be easier to start off to the side of the wood. Then, he said, it would split off into smaller pieces.

I am always willing to at least try what sounds like good advice, and I was getting tired of not making much progress, so . . .

Three hits off to the side and the wood split. A couple more blows to the now smaller piece of wood and it was done.

Wow—if only I had known that before I split the previous ten pieces of wood.

This got me to thinking how I could apply this to Facebook.

Many times, when getting started with Facebook, people will look at everything they need to do and get overwhelmed.

What type of ad are we going to run? What picture are we going to use, or do we want a video? Where am I going to get the picture or video? What headline and copy am I going to use?

I know the feeling you get when you read the list. I got it when I wrote it.

However; if I make a list of what needs to be done step by step and then get started, before long the entire project is done and up and running.

The secret is to take it one chop at a time and making sure that it's in an area that can be accomplished easily. It shouldn't be in the center of the project where it will take a major effort.

Why? Because once the foundational tasks are done the next steps go faster.

How do you pick what to do first? Ask yourself what tasks have to be done before the next ones will work? You need to figure out a sequence and take it step by step.

Sometimes it's all a matter of looking at the challenge with a different set of eyes.

Case Study: Marketing your professional service business via Facebook

Let me tell you about one of my clients, Matthew Wirig of Wirig Orthodontics. Like you, Matthew was skeptical at first. But his desire for growing his business was greater than his fear. He chose to take action and asked me for help.

Matthew had:

- A successful business built with traditional media
- A business Facebook page with over 1200 likes
- No sales coming from Facebook or any other online efforts
- A huge desire to grow a profitable online business page in less than 60 days
- And he wanted a member of his staff, Marshall, to have the knowledge to be able to do this again on their own.

Matthew is an orthodontist in Henderson, Nevada and there are many other orthodontists in the same area who are competing for the same customers.

Matthew's objective: Raise awareness of his practice as THE place to get your children's teeth straightened.

After discussing various options, we set up a variety of offers and ads for their prospects.

Since their audience size is limited because they have a specific geographic area to work in, (after all who is going to travel hundreds of miles to go to an orthodontist?), we planned to rotate different ads and offers to the audience every few weeks so they would always see us, but we would look different when they saw us.

Promotional ideas we used:

- Dentist gives away his Mercedes-Benz in a drawing. You get an entry for every patient you refer to the practice.
- Offer for dentist's book on what you need to know before you get braces for your child's teeth.
- Offer for free consult.

- Promotion of their cool new office which has video games and free ice cream. We had a video tour in the ad.

We worked together to design the first campaign. We went through each of the steps on our checklist (11 Tips For Creating The Ultimate Facebook Marketing Machine) and launched our first campaign. You can get the checklist at www.gosocialexperts.com/11tips

We got limited results the first week, but we did get data about what worked and what didn't, so we made adjustments and got better results.

The next week, when I talked with Marshall, the dentist's marketing person, he had exciting news: The day before, they had gotten their first confirmed patient from Facebook, valued at over $6,000.

This encouraged Marshall to work even harder on his campaigns. A few weeks later, there was another confirmed case from Facebook. In less than 60 days we had the various campaigns up and running.

Matthew, the dentist, now has a marketing person who knows how to use Facebook to produce a steady flow of new business and stay in contact with his existing patients.

He's been able to replicate these results on his own since then and he's thrilled with the results. In fact, Matthew told me when we talked later that he felt I undercharged him for the services.

It's always great to hear that from a client.

Chapter Six

How to Sell Anything to Anyone—on Facebook or Anywhere Else

"When the trust account is high, communication is easy, instant, and effective."
~ Stephen R. Covey

THIS IS A QUOTE and concept I've used many times when teaching people the concept of delivering value before asking for anything in return. I also use this in my own life, including to measure how well I'm doing in my relationships with others.

I first encountered this concept in the mid-'90s. I was a few years behind in getting around to reading Stephen R. Covey's book, *The 7 Habits of Highly Effective People*. It's a great book, if you haven't read it, or if it's been a few years, it's worth reading again.

In the book, Covey uses the concept of an Emotional Bank Account that we have in all our interactions with people. When we do something nice, we put deposits into our account, and when we ask others to do something for us, we withdraw money from our account.

As long as we maintain a high enough balance, we can make withdrawals with no repercussions. It's when we let the balance fall too low that we start to have conflicts and issues.

I look at all my interactions with people through this lens: my family, friends, team members/staff, and the audience of people interested in what I'm selling, including my inactive clients.

Let me share some examples from my life to illustrate this.

I'll start with my staff. When the balance in my account is high enough, and I need them to do extra work, put in extra time, or make extra effort, there's no problem. They dive in to help get things done, and I don't have to use as much of my energy to make a particular project happen. The project just gets done, and we are successful, quickly and easily.

With my friends, it comes down to how willing are they to help when I need help. I don't ask for help often, but you can measure the strength of your relationships by how willing friends are to help you when you ask or to offer to help even before you ask.

When my account balance with my wife is high, I will be excused from helping clean up the dishes so I can finish a project I'm working on, and she might even bring me a cup of coffee to keep me going. When I haven't been tending to the balance and it drops lower, I will get the look that says I never help out around the house. It's the look your spouse gives you when she or he is feeling the weight of the world, and you aren't helping out. This is a sure sign that your account balance is getting low.

What's the sign with kids? When your account balance is high, they are willing to help out around the house or spend time with you. When your balance is low, they move away faster and are reluctant to help.

How about your audience of past customers/clients or patients, or the people who haven't done business with you yet? How is your account balance with them? Do your past clients talk about the great service they got from you and promote you enthusiastically, or do they not mention your business or talk about you only reluctantly? It's your choice. You directly affect how others think of you and your products and services.

Looking at relationships in this way shines new light on why people are willing to listen to you, follow you, help you succeed, and purchase goods or services from you. As long as you're putting regular deposits into your Emotional Bank Accounts, you will move through life getting the help you want and the support you need. As soon as you neglect these deposits, you'll find that your life doesn't flow as smoothly.

One thing to keep in mind is that many of us like to keep saving our money or relational equity and feel bad about making a withdrawal. Don't feel bad about making withdrawals: we need to maintain a positive balance, but that balance is there to use.

After all, your bank doesn't mind you coming in and taking money from your account, no matter how much you want, as long as you've put it in there first. It's your money to spend as you choose.

Your relationship accounts are similar. You've helped people, spent time with them, had fun, and lived, so the equity is there. Don't feel bad about making withdrawals; after all, people want to help you succeed.

Go ahead; take a look at how the people you are interacting with are treating you. Are they willing to help you or do they make constant demands on you and your time? If they are making demands, it's time to get to work and put some deposits into your Emotional Bank Account.

I'll finish this thought with one more quote.

"You can have everything in life you want, if you will just help enough other people get what they want." ~ Zig Ziglar

What does it takes to sell people something using Facebook?

The challenge is that it often takes more effort to get people to invest their time and money than we may expect.

They may love your products and services, they may like you and what you do, but until they actually take the time to read your material or give you money for something, it's just talk.

In my past life, I owned a specialty grocery store. We were known far and wide for our quality meat department. So much so, that despite having been out of the business for over six years now, when I'm in town and people recognize me that they tell me they miss the store and especially the meat department.

The problem with this was that many of them only came to the store once or twice a year, usually when they were having a special event or at the holidays. We were swamped at those times.

The challenge was that our store was inconvenient for these people to get to, so they only made the effort occasionally.

It took me some time to realize that just because people loved our products and store, that they wouldn't always take the time to come buy from us. There were other options that weren't as good, but they were more convenient and they were good enough.

Is this happening in your business? People are giving you great reviews, they tell you that they love your product or service, but yet they aren't spending money with you?

Until people give you money or attention, they are just talking and it doesn't mean anything.

What was surprising to me is how much effort it takes to get people to "buy" from me.

"Buying" can be anything from giving me their email address so I can send them something, to scheduling a free Online Planning Session, to buying one of my books,to purchasing one of our larger coaching products. It's all buying.

I've found that even for my free report I have to keep selling by pointing out what people are going to get from it right up to the time that they download it. Now this doesn't take as much effort as getting them to buy a $5,000 product, but it still takes effort.

When I'm planning the sale of any product, I look at what I'm asking and then plan accordingly. When I'm asking for an email, I may have a paragraph of text or a one or two-minute video. When I'm looking to sell a product valued at $4,000, $5,000, or more, I may have multiple videos, a webinar, and a long sales page all followed up with a call. I put in whatever it takes to sell the item, and make sure to keep selling until they say stop or they purchase.

You never know what will convince someone to buy from you. This is one part of the *11 Tips for Creating the Ultimate Facebook Marketing Machine*. If you don't have it yet get it at www.gosocialexperts.com/11tips and see what steps it takes for you to create your own ultimate Facebook marketing machine.

Just imagine what it will be like in 12 months to have a system in place that automatically brings you a steady flow of prospects and customers on autopilot.

What's your number?

If you're interested in growing your business to a new level, you need an answer to this question: What is your number?

Not long ago, I was at an event where Loral Langemeier presented and she asked this question. To be honest, at first I wasn't sure where she was going with it.

What she was really asking is this: How much do you want to grow your sales from where they are now? More specifically, she was asking, have you narrowed this number down?

For example, let's say your yearly number is $240,000. That's $20,000 a month. $5,000 per week. $1,000 per working day.

Which looks easier, $240,000 or $1,000? The act of breaking it down makes the number look and feel smaller. If you ask me how to generate an extra $240,000 in the next year, that answer is much harder to give than how to generate an extra $1,000 per day.

What's so important about having a specific number to aim at? Isn't the goal of business to earn as much money or generate as many sales as possible?

In the past I used to think so and I worked hard to create as many sales as possible. The problem with this approach is that you have no goal to aim for. You have no extra push when you're close and no feeling of success from reaching your goal.

I've found that when my goal is just a little bit more then what I'm doing or have done I work harder for it. I know I can do it. I want to prove it to myself that I can.

If my goal is so big that my mind won't believe I can reach it, then I'm not going to try my hardest. I may tell others and myself that I'm able to do it and I'm trying. Or the famous, "we got this." But I'm lying to everyone, including myself. In my heart I know it's out of my reach.

That's when breaking the number down to a more manageable goal comes in. It makes it seem more possible. Before you know it, you're reaching your goal numbers and wondering why it was such a big deal to begin with.

The one thing you need to be aware of though is that to reach new and bigger goals, you have to do something different then you did in the past. If not, then your results are going to stay the same.

What are you doing different from last year? How are you going to reach your larger goals?

With this book, I'm suggesting that you look into adding Facebook marketing into your business efforts.

What is your number? What are you going to do differently to reach your number? It's time for you to start reaching your goals.

What KISS can teach you about Facebook

You remember a little rock band from the '80s that wore some crazy leather outfits, painted their faces and constantly stuck their tongues out before Miley Cyrus made it "cool"? That's right—I'm talking about KISS and I went to one of their concerts a few summers ago.

It was my first time seeing KISS live. I knew most of their hit songs but hadn't been a big fan.

My wife wanted to see them and we realized that they may not be touring for many more years so we took advantage of them being in our area.

They put on a great high energy show. What I found interesting is that everyone wanted to hear their old songs. But the thing is, they didn't stop recording albums in the '80s. Their last one was in 2012 and there is even a rumor of a new KISS album in the works. But the songs that get the best crowd response at their shows are their old hits.

So what does this have to do with Facebook?

Well, it seems to me that if classic music is good when you hear it again, how about classic posts and ads you used in the past?

You spent time and effort creating them and they worked well. People did what you asked from the ads and liked, clicked and shared the posts.

Why can't you use them again? If they worked the first time around, why wouldn't they work the next time? I don't know that I would reuse the same post every week, but with tweaks every couple weeks or monthly it could still work.

How do you get away with that? Well, you don't use the exact same post that often. If you had a great picture and a quote that people really responded to, you can reuse it every few weeks. And you can take the quote and put it on other pictures.

Or . . . You take the same picture that worked great and put another quote on it.

Using this strategy, you've got four posts to work with. You only had to create two posts, and you can reuse all of them.

What about an ad? Well first of all, if an ad is performing why stop it? We've had successful Facebook ads run for up to a year or longer with only minimal changes. As marketers and business owners we often get tired of ads before our audience does.

And when a successful ad stops working as well to one audience, you can move it to a different audience and get good results there too. If not, stop it for a couple months and then run it again. Many times, with a break, an ad that had lost its luster comes back performing as well or better than the first time around. There is easy money in the old content you've created.

Develop a system to track how different posts have performed and use the best-performing ones again and again. It's a formula that has kept KISS in their fans' minds for decades. Take that formula and use it in your business.

You do have to keep creating new ads and posts. After all, even KISS is still making new albums after 40 years. However, don't forget about your classics. Make sure to rotate them into your schedule.

By the way, KISS also uses Facebook. They have a Facebook following of over 12,800,000 people. Pretty good for a group of old guys. I can't imagine Gene Simons or Paul Stanley being the ones posting on Facebook. They likely have someone who manages it for them. If you're interested in finding out what it looks like to have someone help you manage your Facebook page, or manage it for you, let's talk.

You can schedule a call with me at www.gosocialexperts.com/callbrian 30. After you schedule the call there will be a few questions for you to answer. Nothing tough.

These questions help me prepare for our call.

Remember KISS has a great rock band and a great Facebook presence. They don't do both; they do what they do best and hire someone for the rest.

Chapter Seven

Selling on Facebook—Things to Keep in Mind

FIRST AND FOREMOST, you need to remember that Facebook isn't an ATM.

Just because you start using Facebook for marketing people aren't going to automatically do what you ask.

They don't turn into mindless robots who do everything you say just because they see your Facebook ad.

If you don't have a good offer that your customers want and you don't have good messaging along with a system to follow up with people who do what you ask, you're not going to make as much money as you could.

Facebook does a great job of finding the people you want to talk to and helping you develop a relationship with them, but then it's up to you to sell to them.

The process you set up is independent of Facebook. Facebook is a great tool for getting your message in front of people, but what happens next depends on how well you've developed your follow-up system.

This follow-up system can use Facebook itself or it can be supplemented by email or even direct mail. This is all part of online marketing.

If you are able to close sales online, great! You can get an introduction, earn your prospect's trust, and collect money without even talking to your customer. The best part is, you can do it quickly—much faster than you can in the "real" physical world.

Even if your business isn't 100 percent online, you still need to feed people into your sales process.

Many businesses can't complete the entire sale online. For example, hairdressers, spas, dentists, chiropractors, car washes, lawn care services and other service businesses operate in a limited area.

Others like consultants, coaches, financial planners, insurance agents, and accountants usually talk to their clients before they even start working with them. (I don't know many people who will hire a consultant without talking to them.) And Facebook can help start that conversation.

All of these businesses can and do use Facebook profitably.

They use Facebook to find people interested in what they offer and then send them to a web page, or to their website, to learn more about them and collect their information so they can follow up.

It's all part of their sales process.

Facebook is a powerful tool that you can profitably use as long as you follow a proven system.

I've created a FREE Online Masterclass for you that goes into detail about what a complete Facebook and Online Marketing System looks like. You can sign up for it at www.gosocialexperts.com/masterclass.

What are you selling?

Let me predict what's happening: You're posting and interacting with people on your Facebook page, but it's not leading to any sales or leads.

This is a common problem for people who haven't learned to sell their services and products effectively using Facebook.

The act of selling doesn't take any longer than not selling. It just requires doing activities in a different order.

What I want to talk about here isn't the process of selling. I want to talk about the very first question that you need to answer if you want to sell anything: What are you selling?

Most of the time, the sales process starts long before you get to the point of asking someone to buy from you.

The key is identifying those steps and developing a system to lead people in a direction that offers them value and brings them closer to buying from you.

So what this means is that we may be "selling" on our sales-oriented Facebook page without asking anyone for money.

What do I mean by that? Well, if we're able to move people to the next step in our selling process by starting on Facebook, we are selling even if this step generates no direct revenue.

Look at it this way. When someone is in the position to hire a Facebook and online marketing expert, they will rarely take that step before talking to the person or company they are considering hiring.

Knowing that, one of the steps in my sales process is to offer a complimentary consultation call where I help you develop a customized Facebook marketing plan. This isn't for everybody, but if you are interested in talking to me, schedule a call at https://www.gosocialexperts.com/callbrian30.

The idea is to use our own success system to generate business for our company. We do this by providing value on our Facebook page and our blog and emails and offering other information to help our followers have success in their Facebook and online marketing. When our followers are ready to take the next step in Facebook marketing they contact us. We talk to them and if we agree that we should work together, we move forward.

At other times, when I'm helping others learn how to implement paid Facebook marketing on their own, I'll talk about my online training program, Smart Facebook Marketing, which trains business owners or their staff how to manage their own Facebook marketing to get fast results. I offer the same value, but instead of offering a free call, I send people to the information page about my course.

In both cases, my Facebook page *is* part of the sales process, but I'm not actually selling anything right on the page.

My challenge to you is to decide what you are selling and then look at your Facebook efforts and see if they're leading people to the next step you want them to take. If they are, congratulations. If not, sit down and lay out a plan so you can get better results.

Are you even comfortable selling?

This question may seem silly, but believe it or not, there are businesspeople who are uncomfortable with the idea of selling.

They know that they need to sell in order to stay in business, but they would rather sales happened on their own without thought or effort.

This objection to selling takes different forms. It may be lack of confidence that your product or services can really help other people. Some business owners don't want to "bother" people.

Whatever the challenge, this attitude is not a recipe for long-term success.

After all, if you're offering a quality product or service that helps people, isn't it your duty to help as many of them as possible?

And if your product or service isn't high quality and doesn't help people, why are you offering it for sale at any price? Make the changes you need and create a product or service you're proud of, then go out and make good things happen. Be on a mission to change the world, at least the part you can reach and help.

After all, nothing happens until something is sold. There is no work to do or activity to pursue until something is sold.

Some business owners know that they need to sell to be successful. They talk about success, but they don't do anything different to change their results. To get different results, you have to take different actions.

So let's look at it another way. Why do people buy what you're selling?

How does your product or service change your buyer's life?

Let's face it. After being in business for multiple years you start to forget what a difference you make to your customers and clients.

You've been selling the same old _____ forever and you'll keep on selling the same old _____ .

But wait a minute. Have you thought about what a difference you make to the people who buy your products?

Everyone is looking for a way to make their lives better. Maybe it's by buying an ice cream cone or hiring a lawyer or hiring an expert to help them with their Facebook marketing. It's your job to tell them why their life is going to be better for having purchased from you.

Some of the biggest reasons people might want to purchase from you are:

- **They're going to have more money from working with you.** Either you save them money on their expenses or you help them increase their income.
- **You've made their lives less stressful.**
- **You've elevated their status.** Does your product make them appear more successful?
- **And last, but certainly, not least . . . you've made their lives easier.** Maybe you gave them more free time with your service? Recently, for example, as I was leaving my house for a meeting, I noticed the lawn care company I hired coming to take care of the lawn. They do a great job and it allows me extra time in the evenings and on the weekends to spend time with my family instead of cutting the grass!

As you take the time to remember why you got into the business you're in, you will see many reasons why people will buy from you.

If you want to take this one step further, ask your customers why they buy from you and make a list of their three or four biggest reasons.

All of this information will help you create compelling messages for your audience—in writing an ad, when you're talking with them, and when you are creating your online marketing campaigns.

After all, everyone likes to have more money, be less stressed, be seen as a positive role model, and have an easier life.

Taking all of this information into account and using Facebook to sell does look a little different from using Facebook for your own enjoyment.

How should you use Facebook to sell?

From time to time, offer your products and services to your Facebook audience. It may be something you sell, an invitation to a webinar or training, an offer for free training in exchange for an email, or an invitation to an event you're hosting. There are many items you can offer that will move people closer to becoming your customer.

The next item your Facebook page needs to nurture an audience is a theme or plan. What kind of content are you posting?

- Is it content you create?
- Is it curated content from multiple sources?
- Are you inspiring people to be better?
- Are you providing guidance?

Whatever you choose, is your audience interested in what you're posting? Do they feel that you're actually trying to help them be successful?

As you can see, there are many possibilities to consider as you develop your sales-oriented Facebook page.

Remember: It's all a mindset. Change your mindset; know that selling is helpful, then develop a plan and start selling using Facebook's formidable power.

Facebook is no exception to the fact that to be successful you have to sell something. It is a powerful tool that can be made to work for you.

If you are wondering where to start harnessing the power of Facebook, you can schedule a *complimentary consultation call* with me at www.gosocialexperts.com/callbrian30 and we'll lay out a plan to get up and rolling easily and effortlessly.

Case Study: Selling your membership program via Facebook

Does your business offer a monthly membership program? If so, would you like more people to subscribe? If you don't currently offer a monthly membership program, you might want to consider offering one.

It's a great feeling knowing that every month you have a consistent income to start the month off with. Let me share what happened with Simone and Duncan's Cutting Horse Training Online. Their story will inspire you.

I met them at an event we were attending. One morning at breakfast, Duncan and I were chatting and he brought up Facebook. He knew what I did and he wanted my opinion. He and Simone had been using Facebook for marketing their business and had built up a nice Facebook fan page, but they weren't getting many sales from their efforts. They were frustrated and they knew there was a better way, but they hadn't been able to find it. They had a successful online business, but it wasn't growing as fast as they knew it could.

We started working together and kicked their Facebook marketing into high gear.

While they had built a Facebook page with over 15,000 likes, they hadn't yet converted them into customers. They also hadn't set up their website to track who came to the site, and weren't building an audience of people that they could send advertisements to on Facebook.

We started with these tactics—targeting their Facebook fans and their website visitors with special offers.

As these audiences accepted the offers, their sales grew. In fact, sales grew faster than expected. They were very pleased!

But their story doesn't end there.

They opted to follow my advice and spend money on very specific Facebook ads that I created.

They were selling monthly memberships for $39/month.

Here's what their campaign looked like:

- They spent $1,000 on Facebook ads.

- They sold $1,200 worth of monthly memberships in 30 days ($200 profit in the first month).
- All of the people who signed up <u>stayed for over a year.</u> So, at the end of the year that $1,000 of Facebook ad spend resulted in $14,400 in sales and counting.

Simone and Duncan are now in control of how fast their company continues to grow. They can turn their growth up or down depending on how many new members they can handle while continuing to serve their existing members.

I won't kid you; creating a sales funnel that generates success at this level does take an investment, both in your time and your money. You don't get this level of success from browsing a few articles and casually running a few ad campaigns. <u>It takes a proven system to make this kind of success happen. Each part of the system builds upon the success of the previous piece, and as you implement each one, your success accelerates.</u>

When they started this process they didn't have any guarantee of success. They just knew that there was a better way, and that they were going to do whatever it took to find out what it was. Simone and Duncan were willing to invest in a system like this and now it's paying off for them.

Chapter Eight

Crafting Your Facebook Sales Campaign

NOT ALL OF YOUR FACEBOOK ADS are going to work. In fact, 7 out of 10 probably won't work, at least not the first time you run them.

Why do I say that?

I'm looking at our results—especially when we start working with a new client—and we are trying to find the messages that resonate with the audience when we start a *new* campaign with a *new* offer.

As we get started, we take what we know; we find the people who we think are most likely to buy from us, and we show them our ads. Sometimes they respond and sometimes they don't.

How do we succeed in spite of that?

I find that it's easier to be prepared ahead of time. We've always worked at creating several ads for a campaign as we are getting going, but originally, we didn't have a system that focused our efforts and organized the process.

What we were doing was working for the most part, but I've been looking for a better way. Several years ago at Digital Marketer's annual Traffic and Conversion Summit, I saw a presentation by Molly Pittman, Digital Marketer's talented traffic manager. She had designed a tool to use when creating a campaign that increases the odds of success 20X.

The idea that Pittman developed is that there are different people, or *avatars*, who might be interested in what you're offering.

Additionally, there are different "hooks" that will work for the different avatars.

In marketing, an avatar is an individual with the characteristics of the people you are targeting with a message. It is your complete picture of the person you think will be interested in your product.

Your "hook" is your marketing message. What in your message is going to hook your avatar's attention so that they want to learn more about what you're offering?

When you take the time to fill out Molly Pittman's tool, you have multiple messages ready for different avatars. Once you start running your ads, you have the material ready to test and use.

This process takes more time to set up as you're getting started, but as you start running your ads and monitoring your results, you can move faster to make adjustments.

I've created a spreadsheet of the tool. I've put it at www.gosocialexperts.com/adgrid and you can download it. No opt-in is required—just take it and use it to improve your Facebook ad results.

You'll notice in row two that there is a place for four different avatars, and down column A is the place to enter your different marketing hooks.

When those are filled out, you have 20 boxes, and in those boxes you put the marketing message you want to use for the particular hook and the avatar that corresponds with it.

This will give you 20 marketing messages to use when you start your campaign.

If you want to attract and connect with different people without spending large amounts of money, then this will be the most important article you read all year.

It's possible to throw money at a marketing problem and increase your response. However, the question is, are you profiting from the response, or do the increased numbers just make you feel good?

I was talking to one of my clients, Steve, a few weeks ago, and he mentioned that he had increased his spending on Google Ads to $250 a day. Although the traffic to this website exploded, he didn't sell any more than he had without spending the extra money. The numbers on the traffic graph that Google displayed just made him feel good. He laughed as he commented that he soon came to his senses as the charges from Google kept climbing and his sales stayed flat.

We want to keep this from happening to you, either with Google or Facebook.

Create your avatar

Let's start with the avatar: What is it, and how do we go about developing one, let alone five?

An avatar is a description of your ideal customer or client—the person you really want to talk to. Usually when you're creating your avatar, you are creating one specific person. It's even better if you name the person and have a picture of that person. You can search for pictures on Google and find one that matches who you're targeting.

In this process, you are looking for as many different people as possible who might be interested in your offering. These might be different than an avatar you have for your company as a whole.

Let's look at one of my offers. *11 Tips for Creating the Ultimate Facebook Marketing Machine.* Go to www.gosocialexperts.com/11tips to get it.

For this example, I'll use the people who might be interested in this report:

- The owner of a larger business.
- A marketing manager for a larger business.
- The person doing the social media work for a business.
- A solo entrepreneur.
- A freelancer.

Next, we need marketing hooks we can use. What is a hook, you ask? It's a message that catches a person's attention so they want to find out more about your product.

What kind of hooks may catch the attention of my avatars? How about:

- Are your Facebook marketing efforts profitable?
- Attract a steady flow of new customers to your business.
- Build a predictable Facebook marketing machine that brings you consistent results.

- Are you missing any of these in your Facebook marketing plan? Download and evaluate your Facebook marketing efforts.
- Are you getting a good ROI on your Facebook marketing?

Once you have filled out the avatars and the hooks, there are now the boxes in the middle of the grid that you'll fill in with different marketing messages.

The owner of the company is going to have a different interest in evaluating the company's social media efforts as opposed to the person doing the work, or the freelancer who is doing everything themselves.

It does take some time to fill all of these boxes in, but it's work done ahead of time. It sets you up to succeed faster; if one message isn't working you have other ones ready to go.

The second tab on the spreadsheet is set up for your results. You take the results you got from the different ads after letting them run for five days, and then fill in the squares in the appropriate box on the grid.

This gives you an easy way to compare the performance of the different avatars and hooks and lets you see which you need to stop or adjust as well as which ones to expand your spending on.

Taking the time to set up the ad grid will lead you to profits faster than throwing up a few ideas and starting to run an ad.

You make real profits on Facebook when you use a complete system. Running an ad, making a few sales, and moving on feels good, but if you want to grow your company, you need to be constantly growing and improving your results. When you use a system, this happens.

The Hook – what it is and why you NEED it.

You have an incredible picture that stops people scrolling dead in their tracks. Your headline makes them read the ad, and you have killer copy in the text, but you're not getting any results...

What's wrong?

You might be missing *the hook.*

What's a hook? You ask, as a friend did the other day when I asked him for a hook on a project we are working on together.

A hook is a message that grabs someone's attention and won't let them go until they have read the article.

It's like a fishhook with bait that grabs a fish's attention and won't let him go until you bring him in or let him go. Or that lyric from the latest pop song that just will not stop playing on repeat in your head.

A powerful hook will substantially increase the number of people who do what you ask them to do. Not just in your ads, but also in your posts and emails. Basically, anywhere you communicate with people.

What's your endgame?

When you're writing a Facebook ad (or any ad, really) you need to know what you want someone to do before you even start.

Basically, what is your endgame? Should they click, read more, share your post, buy your product and change their life?

Once you have this down you can start developing your hook.

During this stage, don't worry so much about the wording. Just focus on figuring out what you want them to do.

Once you've identified your call to action, you can develop that concept into a hook that baits them into doing what you ask.

Creating your hook

Do some research before getting creative:

- Research why your current customers are buying from you.
- Ask why your past customers bought from you.
- Use Amazon as a research tool. How are best-selling books in your niche being marketed?
- Search Google for similar products to yours. How are they being marketed?
- Why are you offering this particular item or service?
- What are the benefits of the item or service? Is there anything hidden in this list?

- What is your unique selling point (USP)? What is the USP of the product?

Ask yourself what would make your ideal customer do what you'd like them to do. Is there an emotion they'd like to feel? A result they're looking for?

Use your research and your answers to those questions to develop your hook.

Here are some examples of hooks that others have used:

- Federal Express – "When it absolutely, positively, has to be there overnight"
- One-Legged Golfer – "Amazing Secret Discovered By One-Legged Golfer Adds 50 Yards To Your Drives, Eliminates Hooks and Slices…And Can Slash Up to 10 Strokes From Your Game Almost Overnight!"
- Cosmopolitan Magazine – "50 Ways to Thrill A Man – Warning By #18 He'll Barely Remember His Name"
- 4-Hour Workweek – "The 4-Hour Workweek: Escape 9-5, Live Anywhere, and Join the New Rich"

As you can see, there is some work involved in creating a good marketing hook. It may take some time to develop, but once you find it you'll find the effectiveness of all of your marketing improves.

You'll find, just like any other skill you practice, that creating hooks gets easier with time.

If you would like help in developing a hook, (since many times an outsider has fresh eyes) I have a 1-2-1 Strategy Session available that would be perfect for this. In 45 min we can talk about creating a great hook (or work on any other question you may have about Facebook advertising) and get you on the right track to success. Sometimes, just bouncing ideas around with someone is priceless. But in this case, you're bouncing ideas around with an expert in the industry who has years of experience creating hooks that work. Go to www.gosocialexperts.com/coaching to schedule your call.

Remember, you're talking with real people

I've seen this far too often: I will be talking with a business owner and he or she will expect instant, predictable results.

They desire a guarantee that if we do A, doing more of A will make 'it' better. Their question is, will our ROI stay the same as we increase our spending?

The answer is: *sometimes*. I know that's frustrating to hear. I'm frustrated to have to say it. The challenge is that we're talking about people.

Many times marketers, writers, or business owners forget that we're talking about real people when we're making marketing plans and analyzing the numbers.

We look at our audiences as lists of emails, Facebook likes, Facebook interests, readers, etc. We know how big our email list is, how many likes we have on Facebook—so how many people can we reach with our ads?

What we often miss is that there are real people behind all of these numbers.

A name on an email list is a real person. A Facebook fan is a real person and an audience of interests on Facebook is a group of real people.

When we try and predict what they are going to do, that's all we're doing—predicting. We can have the best data, put our best efforts forward, and *still* not get the results we expect.

Sometimes our results are better than expected; sometimes they aren't what we planned for. Because one group of people responded a certain way, you can't assume that another is going to respond the same way.

This brings me to a discovery I made many years ago myself, and it's what stops many people from going into business or pursuing other dreams:

You can make all the best predictions, create great plans, and gather the best people, but the only way to know if they work is to implement them.

Many times the implementation costs time and money. You have to pay to find out if it works. Depending on the scale of the project, it may be a few dollars to millions of dollars. Until you're willing to get out your checkbook and go all in, you'll never know if your idea will work.

The same is true for Facebook marketing. You can make great plans with engaging web pages, content, and ads but until you actually run the ads, you won't see any results.

So here is my advice: Take the time to put together the best plan you can, hire the best people you can afford to implement your plans, and *get started*.

Remember, every name on your list, every Facebook like, and every reader of your blog is a real person. Treat them as such and watch your results change.

Chapter Nine

Get Their Contact Info

THERE IS A PROVEN FORMULA that you can use to market your business on Facebook. One of the key advantages of this system is that you and your staff won't have to spend hours on Facebook to get great results.

The steps are:

1. Create a sales-oriented Facebook page.
2. Find your ideal audience.
3. Deliver value before asking for a sale.
4. Get your audience's contact information.
5. Market to those people (i.e., sell them something).

Let's talk about number four.

Why do we want their contact information?

In my *Success System for Facebook* I use the example of meeting someone at a networking event and getting to know them before asking for their card. When we go our separate ways—if we've connected—we exchange contact information, usually in the form of business cards. On most cards, you'll see your contact's name, company name, phone number, email, address, etc.

We're looking to do this online. Interaction online mirrors the physical world more and more each year. However, we need to use different tactics to accomplish this positive interaction. We don't have a business card in the online world to trade like we do in face-to-face meetings. Online, our audience has already found us and doesn't need any further information to contact us.

Another issue we need to consider online is that we always want more than one way to connect with our audience.

Think about it this way. We mentioned that on a business card we get our new friend's name, address, email, phone number, and company information. We can return home and connect with them on LinkedIn, friend them on Facebook, and follow them on Twitter with this information. We can also mail them a thank you card, call them, or send them an email. We have a wide range of possible points of contact; we aren't limited to one way to follow up with them.

We need to keep in mind that the most dangerous number for our business interactions is the number one. If we only have one way to connect with our prospective customers, we are at risk of losing access to the one way. Where would our business be? I've had clients in the past two years lose access to large email lists or lose their Facebook ad accounts and have to start over. They were barred from sending direct mail due to industry challenges and even had to deal with Google changing its algorithms, sending their website traffic into a nosedive.

The responses we receive from our audience are also better if we have more than one way to connect with them.

Think about it this way. If you receive an email from me, you may or may not open it. However, if you see an email subject line—even if you don't open the actual email—an impression is made on your mind. Then, let's say, you're on Facebook and you see a similar message in a post and you go "mmm." Then you see another Facebook post or a second email. Now my message is starting to reach you. What you do next depends on your preference; do you open one of the emails or click on the Facebook post? Offering those options will help my business grow faster.

Another advantage to having a person's email is that it's cheaper to reach them. While Facebook ads aren't expensive, they do cost more money than an email would. If you can reach your audience at a lower cost, there is a benefit. Millions of dollars are made via email consistently day after day, year after year.

Another way to connect that's not often talked about is by sending a card or package in the mail. Imagine the surprise and delight your new subscriber will feel when they receive a package in the mail from you. What will that do to your response rate? You might want to consider testing this.

So what's stopping us from collecting all of this information?

Why can't we find more than one way to connect with our audience online?

We can if we structure our offers correctly.

If we do a great job providing value before we ask for potential client's information, then it would make sense to them to provide us with it.

Remember, the more options we can utilize to stay connected to our audience, the more secure and profitable our business will be.

Do i ask for everything I want or just what I need?

The challenge we have online is that the more information we ask for, the less people are willing to sign up for our offer—and we really want those signups.

Or do we? When we get large amounts of unqualified sign-ups—people less likely to purchase our products—we spend time and money marketing to prospects who may not be the types of customers we want. Some customers aren't profitable for you. Do you really want to work with them?

You have to choose what you want from your results: Do you want a large number of potential customers or a smaller, more qualified contact list? The correct answer depends on the goal of your campaign. I've used both and have achieved good results from both strategies.

One of the filtering techniques you can use is asking for all the information up front. You'll know that if people fill it all out, they are committed to working with you, versus just providing their first names and email addresses.

A possible way to compile a large number of contacts and collect information is to just ask prospective customers for their name and email for a digital download. Then on the next page, offer to send a physical copy to them, and ask for their physical address. This is a way to have your cake and eat it too. And this indicates to you which customers are most interested in your offer.

What do we offer to give them in exchange for their address?

In person we give prospective customers our business cards; online they already have our contact information. Now what?

The best strategy is to give them information that is even more valuable or is a continuation of what we had been talking about in our free information. Some call this type of content a *lead magnet*.

A lead magnet is something that we give people to encourage them to give us their contact information. Ideally when they read, watch, or listen to it, they are interested in doing business with us. It draws people to us who are interested in what we do and repels people who aren't interested in what we do.

When you offer a lead magnet in addition to offering a product or service, it gives people a reason to say: I may be interested in your products or services, just not yet. When you have the information they provide once offered the lead magnet, you have a chance to follow up with these people and sell to them once they're ready.

Some ideas for lead magnets are:

- Online Lead Magnets
  1. Audio download/Audio Book
  2. E-book
  3. Free course membership site
  4. Email course
  5. Report or white paper, PDF download
  6. Video (one or a series of videos)
  7. Free webinar
- Get Physical Address
  1. Printed book
  2. Printed report or white paper

   3. CD (yes some people still listen to these)
   4. DVD (yes some people watch these on their TV as well as on their computer)
- Get them to come to your store or arrange a face-to-face interaction.
   1. Coupon or discount offer
   2. Free gift that they have to stop in to pick up
   3. Use an online scheduler for your prospect to schedule an appointment
   4. Free gift when you schedule an appointment
   5. Free gift when you show up for an appointment
- Get Phone Number
   1. Complimentary call
   2. Discovery call
   3. Fill out form and follow up with a call

As you can see, there is a wide variety of ways to encourage people to give you their contact information. If you've done a good job of giving them value first, they will be eager to give you their information so that you can help them even more.

People are at different stages in their relationship with you

One issue of which you need to be aware is that each of the different lead magnets we listed require different levels of commitment from your audience. If you haven't provided enough value before you ask your audience for their information, they aren't going to want to give you anything.

As we discussed earlier, in his book, *The 7 Habits of Highly Effective People,* Stephen Covey talks about the Emotional Bank Account that we have in all of our relationships. When we do nice things for people, we make a deposit into our accounts, and when we ask them to do something for us, or we forget their birthday or our anniversary, we make a withdrawal. As long as our balance is above zero—the higher, the better—everything will go smoothly. As soon as our balance drops low or below zero, our relationship will be rougher.

As businesspeople, we have that same kind of relationship with all of our customers. When we give them value or items they value our balance increases; when we ask them to do anything, including giving us their contact information or buying something, our balance declines. As long as our balance is high enough, our relationship is solid and people are willing to do what we ask, but as soon as it drops below zero we have to rebuild the balance.

If our balance is high enough, people will give us anything we want, including money. We just need to make sure that we keep our account balance high.

Many of the items on my list above require a substantial withdrawal from your account, so they may not be suitable for the first time someone sees your offer. You will have to measure where your people are in their relationship with you.

How do we decide what to offer?

Depending on what we want from our prospects, we design what we are giving them accordingly.

If we want their physical address, we need to offer to send them something of value in the mail.

If we want only their email address, we offer them a digital download.

If we want them to come to our store, we offer them a discount or a gift with their purchase.

If we want them to schedule an appointment, we offer a gift when they schedule or when they come in for their appointment.

If we want to get their phone number, we offer a complimentary discovery call or a problem-solving call or its equivalent.

One other solution is to ask for the information ahead of time, but not make the extra fields required. This will get you the information from the people willing to share it and still give the others a chance to indicate interest.

Just remember that some of your readers will not even try to fill in the information if they see a long list of questions when they start to fill in the form.

As I mentioned above, we can two-step this and offer the digital download first, then offer to send a physical item and ask for more information. In that way, we still get the majority of people who come to the page, but we will collect more information from them.

If you have a highly successful page and have done the work of giving people information ahead of time, 20 percent or more of people will fill out the information

What do you do with the rest of the people?

Are they lost? No, they're not. For whatever reason, they're just not ready to share their information yet.

You collect them in an audience using the Facebook retargeting pixel, a small piece of code that lets you show Facebook ads to people who triggered the pixel. Then you tell Facebook you want to show these people an ad.

You give these people more information about your products and services. As you give them more and more information, you'll be adding deposits to your emotional bank account and growing the balance

Keep at it and sooner or later they will give you their contact information. At that point, they'll be one step closer to becoming customers.

It's our job to stay in front of our audience, not their job to remember us.

Many times as business owners we expect people to just remember us. We spend our lives in our business and subject, and it consumes us. Why doesn't that happen to our audience?

Many times this is because as business owners it takes work to follow up with people and stay connected.

I've been guilty of this myself. It's all too easy to expect my audience to be as interested as I am in Facebook and online marketing—what changes there are and what the changes can do for them.

That's just not true. After all, not many people spend forty hours or more a week talking and thinking about Facebook and online marketing.

This means I need to have a plan to put this information and more in front of anyone who has expressed interest in Facebook and online marketing.

I do that with email, my blog, and Facebook. You'll find Facebook articles consistently on these various platforms, as well as marketing ideas and examples of good and bad experiences that I or one of my friends have had.

To see what a complete Facebook marketing system looks like, register at www.gosocialexperts.com.masterclass. You'll get five videos over the next five days walking you through my five step process.

Case Study: Using Facebook to fill your events

As you know, when you get people to come together live, you have the best chance of helping them and influencing them to take action.

The challenge is getting people to commit to coming to a live workshop.

After all, they must work the event into their schedule, rearrange their other errands, and if they have families this is even harder.

Let me tell you about one of the people for whom we regularly help fill local workshops.

Dr. Woods is an MD and a functional medicine provider. She knows that the more people she reaches, the more people she can help live healthier, fuller lives.

She offers monthly workshops on specific topics that her community is interested in. These workshops enable her to find the people who need her help and who might become patients in the future.

We regularly get between 60 and 80 registrants for each event. How do we get those numbers?

We use Facebook advertising. Along with filling her workshops, we're helping her create an email list and a Facebook audience. With every event she has, she is growing her audience, making each follow-up event less expensive to target and promote.

The first thing we need is a hot title. One that will attract people interested in the topic, and it needs to be Facebook-friendly too. In the medical field, this is particularly important.

Next comes the copy. What do we say to entice interested people to consider attending this event?

Along with the copy, we need to have a picture that grabs our audience's attention or a video that tells them what the event is about and what benefits they're going to get from attending.

Videos have been working well to get people signed up for our events.

Who do we target? We want to show our ads to people who are most likely to accept our invitation. With Facebook's many targeting options we have many choices. When targeting for events, for example, we use location targeting to target only people within a specific distance from the event location.

We follow the targeting with a well-executed Facebook ad campaign. This includes everything from setting up the proper tracking, choosing the best objective for the campaign, and setting up the retargeting ads for people who expressed interest but haven't signed up yet.

The final step is setting up a registration page that will convince people who click on the ad to sign up. We've been using Eventbrite for this purpose and it has been working well.

Done properly these steps bring down the cost of each registrant, and if you skip any part of this you will end up paying more money for fewer registrants.

With all of this in place, Dr. Woods has been able to consistently fill two to three workshops a month with interested people.

You are probably wondering how much it costs her to do this. The average cost per registrant is $10 to $20 each, depending on the topic she chooses and the day of the week the event is held on; and yes, the day of the week does make a difference.

Live workshops have now become a key part of her practice. She gets to help many people with the information she shares and some of the people she helps move on to become patients.

This strategy can be used in many different industries. The medical, chiropractic, dental, and financial planning industries have used live seminars for years to attract people with great information and then offer them other services to help the attendees get the results that they want.

Chapter Ten

Creating the Perfect Facebook Ad

YOU'VE GOT A MARKETING SYSTEM set up—your ad targeting is dialed in and your Facebook ad is part of a system, right?

In this chapter I want to reveal to you six critical steps for creating Facebook ads that SELL.

Step One: Know what you want to accomplish.

Defining this is critical to the success of the ad. A good Facebook ad will look like a regular post. And when it's done, it'll have brought in shares, comments, and likes for the post and your page. Not to mention all the leads and sales it'll generate for your brand.

There are multiple types of ads that you can choose to use depending on your goals for your campaign:

- Video ads
- Carousel ads (multiple pictures and links in one ad)
- Link click ads (one picture and one link) *most common type of ad*
- Lead Ads

All of these work well and using a variety of these ads is key to building a long-term successful Facebook campaign.

Step Two: Get the picture right.

To create a high-performing Facebook ad, you need to remember that there is one critical difference between it and any other advertising medium you may be used to.

The single most important part of the Facebook ad is the picture.

The picture's job is to stop a reader who is scrolling through their newsfeed and get them to read the post/ad.

If you don't get your reader to stop scrolling through their newsfeed, you don't get a chance for them to take the next step.

What makes a good picture?

The first consideration: what does the web page you're sending the people to look like? You want a similar look and feel in your ad as you have on your web page.

You want your pictures, headline, and text in the ad to be similar to the landing page. This will show your readers that they are in the right place.

Some ideas for what makes a good picture for a Facebook ad:

- People (Especially attractive people)
  - o Make sure they are people about 10 years younger than the age you are targeting
  - o The subjects should be looking at you, making eye contact
- Kids (If they work in with what you are promoting)
- Animals are always good
- High contrast colors in the pictures
  - o Use at least a hint of red in the picture for best results
- Bright green is also a good color to try. It stands out in the newsfeed.
- Avoid blue (Facebook's colors). You will blend in if you use it.

Step Three: Look trustworthy.

This is often overlooked. Just like in an email, who it comes from and the relationship they have with you is the most important factor in getting an email opened. So the page promoting the post is just like the sender field in an email.

Your reader has stopped scrolling and now at the top of the ad is the name of the page and your profile picture. Does it look good to them and resonate with your reader? Do they trust you?

Step Four: Have a killer headline.

You've created a picture that stops your ideal reader in their scroll and they decide that they are willing to take a look at what you have to say. Now you need to get them ready to move to the next step.

You only have a few seconds for this and it's the headline's job to grab their attention right away.

The headline is the bold and larger print below the picture. Does it grab your readers' attention and make them want to read the rest of the ad?

If you want to study writing headlines take some time at the grocery store and look at all the magazines at the checkout counters. These magazines sell by how well their headlines grab attention. Use formulas from there to write your headlines.

Step Five: Write engaging copy.

You are well on your way! Now the next step is the text above the picture. This text shows up no matter what device the reader is using.

The first two or three lines of this section form another headline for your ad. If these lines don't keep your readers attention they won't read any farther.

A quick note, in most cases 70-plus percent of your Facebook traffic is coming from mobile devices. People use them to keep up to date on Facebook more than computers.

You need to give enough information to encourage your readers to do what you want them to do. Sometimes this takes one line and others it takes an entire page of text. Yes, you can use an entire blog post as a Facebook post. We have and in the right situations, we've had great results.

Many times, if you are sending people to another page, you can use information from that page to create your ad. It gives the reader a sense that they are in the right place when they get to the page.

If you're not sending people to another page, you need to make sure your first sentence keeps their attention so they keep reading The problem isn't with the length of the text; it's with how engaging the text is. Does your audience find your writing entertaining or interesting in any way?

Make sure near the end of the text you have a call to action. What do you want your audience to do? Call you? Click here? Go to a web page? Email you? Make sure you spell it out—don't assume your audience will know what you want them to do.

Step Six: Round it out with a great newsfeed description.

The final step of your ad is filling out the newsfeed description. This is the area under the headline. It is limited to 200 characters.

When you're creating your ad this shows up and looks like it will be read.

The challenge is that this only shows up on desktop or laptop computers, not on mobile devices, so most of your traffic won't see this writing.

If you don't put anything in this area, it will pull in any information you have on the landing page you're sending people to.

You can change it to anything you want; just don't spend lots of time on it. An effective idea is to summarize the longer text above in this area.

Finishing up

There are many other parts to a successful ad. You have to test to see what makes a difference. No one knows for sure how an ad will perform to an audience until the ad is run.

A few other issues to consider:

- Are you going to use Facebook's Call to Action button? This is the button that Facebook lets you chose that tells people what to do or expect, learn more, sign up, download, shop, etc.
- What is your offer?
- What objective are you going to use? When getting started use, Traffic, conversion engagement or video views as your fall back options until you have more experience.
- What are acceptable results for you? How much can you spend for a lead or a sale?

This leads me into one last point. Make sure you're measuring the results you are getting.

Facebook gives you data and stats—in fact, more than you can use. Make sure you're tracking your results and more importantly the results that matter. Know where your money is going and how much it's returning to you.

As you can see, there is both a science and an art to creating successful Facebook ads. The challenge is that to be profitable using Facebook, writing a great ad is only one step of the system.

Chapter Eleven

Data Collection and Retargeting

DO YOU HAVE THE FACEBOOK PIXEL on your site and is it working properly? Can you make changes to it easily or do you have to get IT involved?

One of the challenges of being a marketer is that many times you don't have easy access to your website coding and if you did you wouldn't know how to make changes without affecting your site.

A powerful tool that will help you make changes to Facebook Pixels and many others is the GoogleTag Manager at the same time. But what is Google Tag Manager?

Well, I'm glad you asked. . .

Tags are snippets of code, provided by a third party such as Google Analytics. Nearly all of today's digital marketing solutions—including analytics, site personalization, and affiliate marketing—require tags. Tags help you measure traffic, track visitor behavior, gauge the efficacy of social media and online advertising, target audiences, and test your site. Google Tag Manager manages all of this information for you and tracks it within Google Analytics and the appropriate software. You'll find your Facebook numbers in your Facebook ads manager your Google Analytics in your Google Analytics account . . .

So what does this have to do with Facebook?

It takes the same amount of effort to put the Google Tag Manager on your website as it does to install the Facebook Pixel, and once it's on your site, you can make changes to the Pixels on your own in most cases.

If you're running ads on Facebook and don't have a Facebook pixel in place on your website, you're losing out on a ton of data and information. You're literally throwing away everything you need to gauge your ROI along with missing the opportunity to tell Facebook exactly who you are looking for, which reduces your ad costs.

Like I said, now is the time to get all of this set up on your website. The bugs have been worked out, the kinks have been un-kinked, and valuable data is waiting for you.

Even if you don't look at the data for months, it will be there waiting for you, and without data you can't make good decisions.

Retargeting

If you want to use digital marketing *profitably* in your business this may be the most important concept you need to know about.

The secret to making money online is to use retargeting on your website, any sales pages you use, and any web page you have control of.

So the number one question I get is: *What is retargeting?*

It is the ability to track a person who goes to your website and then talk to them again. Think of it like this . . . Someone comes to one of your web pages and you stick a piece of gum on their shoe. No matter where they go, they bring you with them but they don't notice that you're there. They can come to your website on their phone and then see an ad of yours on their tablet or PC. You can track them across any device.

The other way to look at retargeting is to think of it like this . . .

You're driving down the highway and see a billboard for a company. Then a few minutes later on the radio, you hear an ad for the same company. When you get home you check your mail and there is a postcard from the same company. And then as you're watching the evening news you see a TV ad for the same company. What do you think? Are you likely to notice all of these ads for the same business in a short time frame?

With retargeting on Facebook you can accomplish the same thing only at a lot lower cost.

No matter how a person with a Facebook account gets to your website you add your pixel to their Facebook account and you show them ads on Facebook.

These people can come to your website from an organic search, a paid Google ad, from a Facebook ad, or from seeing your website on your vehicle or any other place you're advertising your web address.

So why is this important?

It helps you use online media to create a relationship with people interested in your products and services as well as maintain a relationship with people who have already bought from you.

In my experience, it's rare that someone buys from me when they first meet me or see me in person (though a few do).

They want to get to know me find out what I do and then find out if they like me and if I'm trustworthy. Basically, will I do what I say?

All of this trust develops over several encounters. They get to know me. They find out that I do know what I'm talking about and do what I say I will.

In the past with online marketing, you had to get someone's email to follow up with them. Then you had to develop this level of relationship. But if they didn't opt in (give you their email) and just hand over their information to you, you were out of luck.

This is no longer the case. Using only retargeting, you can develop an entire path for your website visitors, that you send to them over time,.

In other words, you can take someone from "This is my first visit" to "Here is my credit card, PLEASE TAKE MY MONEY"—all without getting their contact information before you get the order.

Not that you shouldn't try and get their email address too, and no, you're not bothering them if you email them with good information. Good information is more than just specials and deals.

Using retargeting means that you control how often people see you.

They don't have to remember to come back to your website. You can reach out to them when you want.

You can develop a relationship with them and when THEY decide it's time to buy, YOU will be the first one they think of.

Imagine what having this set up on your website can do for your business . . .

- You can bring your website from being an expense to being an income generator.
- You have the power to decide what you sell and when you sell it and how much you sell of an item.
- You don't have to rely on email alone to move the sales needle.

If you would like help setting up this entire process, you can schedule a complimentary consultation call at www.gosocialex-perts.com/callbrian30. We'll discuss the details of what you want to accomplish and agree on a price to get it done. You can have this system up and running in short order.

With this information you can now change how your ads talk to people based on what they already know of you from your website.

What does this look like? How can you put this to work for you?

Is your visitor a new prospect or an existing customer? Are they a newbie or an experienced pro?

You can talk to them about exactly what they were looking at on a specific webpage.

This means that if you're selling shoes, you can talk to the person on the page about the exact pair of shoes they looked at.

You can even choose to target people based on how many times they visited the page and how long they stayed on the page. These are some advanced strategies but they can be set up for you and bring you some extraordinary results.

More retargeting tools

Retargeting is the single most profitable tool you can use when marketing online.

Advanced tools let you take retargeting and refine its use. While the basic retargeting is powerful, these tools amp up your results to another level.

You can talk to the people most interested in what you're talking about on your web page based on how many times someone visited or by how long they spent on the page.

After all, if someone spends 10 minutes investigating the pair of shoes that are on the page you are tracking, aren't they more interested than the person who was on the page for 30 seconds?

With this knowledge, you can design your follow-up messages in more detail.

You can ignore the people who spent little or no time on your site and save money while spending the extra effort on those most likely to buy. You can track who bought and exclude them from seeing any more ads, or you can show them ads for products that complement what they bought.

This will make your visitor feel like you're talking to them and not just everyone.

You do have to be careful not to freak out your website visitors with too much tracking and knowledge of what they've done.

After all, people don't want to be aware of how much of their online activities can be monitored, but they do want to get the results from this monitoring.

When you design a customer value path for everyone who visits your site, and connect with them around exactly what they're interested in, you're going to find your sales growing effortlessly.

After all, most businesses aren't willing to put the time and effort into designing an entire system to follow up with people who have visited their site. It is work and takes some thought to design the plan and the messages you send out to get the best results.

As Henry Ford said, *"Thinking is hard work and that is why so few people do it."*

Case Study: Using Facebook to get a fast start with a new product or service

One of my clients, <u>Metropolis Resort in Eau Claire, Wisconsin</u>, has opened several new attractions. The lessons that we've learned have helped us to open each new attraction with lines of people ready to try them out.

The lessons learned are applicable even to those businesses that aren't in an industry that is obviously interesting to large groups of people. Read to the end for ideas on how your business can use these lessons.

Back in December of 2016, Action City, a family fun center and part of the resort, opened a new trampoline park. This was a 30,000 sq. foot expansion filled with trampolines and a large play area for younger kids. (If you haven't been to a trampoline park, you need to check one out.)

Then, over the winter, they built a 135-ft. tall zipline and an outdoor go-cart track. They already had indoor go-carts, as the weather in Wisconsin doesn't allow for outdoor go-carts year-round. We used a similar strategy for each of these openings.

We used their social media following to start a buzz about the opening as it was announced. We used every resource we could. We sent out a press release and when the press did a story about it, we used that on Facebook.

This strategy works well. Anytime you are on TV and can get the clips to use on Facebook you're going to get great exposure.

We also created a sign-up page to capture emails in order to keep the people who were most interested informed of the progress. We had several hundred people signed up before we opened.

During the construction, we kept the public up to date with a steady stream of pictures and posts enabling them to watch the construction as it happened.

As the opening got closer we created videos to show what was coming, and to keep people in the know about what was happening. These videos got a large number of likes, comments, and shares, and raised the excitement in the area.

All of this was designed to raise awareness and excitement in the community, and it enabled Action City's trampoline park to open with crowds of people.

Once the trampoline park opened we followed up with more videos announcing the opening. We also emailed everyone who signed up over the course of the construction, and sent targeted ads to everyone who had interacted with our Facebook posts.

This strategy allowed Action City to exceed the sales projections for the new attractions.

We followed a similar strategy when their outdoor go-cart track and zipline opened.

Now you ask, how can I use this? I'm not launching or starting anything as exciting as a 30,000 sq. foot trampoline park or as exciting as a 135-ft. tall zipline.

No, most of us don't have attractions like that to offer, but you can use a similar strategy.

You can announce what you're doing and offering. You can create a buzz. If you don't feel a press release is warranted, you can use your social media pages to amplify what you're doing, with or without a press release.

You can create videos or informational posts. We've found videos to be effective in many different markets, but I understand that video can be intimidating.

You can create excitement around the opening or official release of your product or service.

There is nothing stopping any of us from reaching out to the entire world with the tools readily available to us via social media, our computers, and smartphones.

Chapter Twelve

Life Lessons:
What Can Your Church Teach You
About Marketing?

"Make your marketing so useful people would pay you for it."
—Jay Baer

ARE YOU ACTIVE in your church—any church or faith community? Why or why not?

That's something to think about. The purpose and main goal of most churches is to help people live better lives, either by helping them out when life gets hard, or by providing spiritual teachings to help them improve themselves. It doesn't matter what religion we're talking about. If you look deep enough, this is the purpose of any church, mosque, or synagogue.

Why are churches struggling? Google that and you get 22,000,000 results. There must be a problem somewhere. And this is an institution dedicated to doing good in the world.

Why aren't you active on a regular basis at your church? If all were well, you would be—after all, churches are dedicated to helping people.

How about your business? Is it struggling or thriving? Are you dedicated to doing good in the world? Are your key precepts as obvious or widely known as those of your church?

I want to suggest that most church struggles and business struggles are related.

The challenge is that the church and your business don't have a share of your target market's mind. Neither is providing value to their audience in a way that the audience cares about.

Have you looked around? Do you realize how many constant distractions there are in the world?

How many people do you know who don't have a smart phone? I know only a handful, and their numbers are getting smaller every month.

Think of the effect this has on people. It gives them constant entertainment at the push of a button. Smart phones have more options to draw you in than I can count.

Look at how it's affected parenting. Many babies are playing with tablets and can access their favorite apps before they're two, or even younger.

What about young adults? We all know the stories of them living on their phones; we witness this as we see a group of them in the same room, all texting—or, more likely, Snapchatting—each other.

We think it stops there, but no.

The other night at dance class, my wife and I arrived a few minutes early, and I looked around. Over 60 percent of the people there were on their phones, not talking to the person they were with or to anyone else. The average age of these people was well into the mid-forties. The phones know no age limit.

What does this have to do with churches and your business? Well, what are you doing to combat this? Or how are you using this to your advantage?

This holds true for a church or any nonprofit organization, just like it's true for your business. If a church or nonprofit stops reaching out to people and staying in front of its supporters, it is going to start declining.

It's even more true for a business. If you don't have a plan in place to stay relevant to your customers and prospects in a way they want to be reached, you will soon find your business declining.

It's no fun to be forgotten—and yes, I'm talking from experience, both in business and over my many years of involvement in my church as it has cycled through many challenges.

Most of your customers aren't thinking of you as an institution devoted to doing good in the world; they are thinking of you as a business that can help them solve their problem. When you do, you're a hero; when you don't, you're a bum.

Develop a plan to stay in front of your customers affordably. Make sure that you're strengthening your relationship with everyone in a way that you can sustain, and watch your business grow.

Ignore this and watch your business decline.

One way that you can stay in front of all those people on their smartphones is to use Facebook, both organically and with paid marketing.

When I look at the reports for most of my clients, I'm seeing that, in most industries, over 86 percent of the traffic comes from phones. With the proper strategies, you can place great content in front of your target audience, and start and maintain great relationships.

If you want some ideas about how to get started using Facebook for your business—or your church, if you're so inclined—set up a complimentary consultation call and we'll talk together for 30 minutes on a Facebook and Online Marketing Planning Session designed for you and your situation. Go to www.gosocialexperts. com/callbrian30 to access my calendar and schedule your time.

If you want to know how to get results with very little tech needed, you want to spend limited money, and you work with people in a limited area, I can help you. If you want to design an elaborate multi-step system that shepherds people from "I just met you" to "Here's my credit card please take my money" on a nationwide or worldwide scale, I can help with that—and everything in between.

What Paul McCartney Can Teach You about Building Your Audience

Remember Paul McCartney? I mean seriously, how could you forget?

This musical genius started making music in 1950s, was the co-lead vocalist and bassist for the Beatles, and is still going strong as a singer, songwriter, musician, composer, and record and film producer.

Considering that Paul McCartney is now in his 70s it's also safe to say that this guy is no spring chicken. And yet . . . he has quite the following.

- *Facebook Fans: 6.9 million**
- *Twitter Followers: 4 million*
- *Instagram Followers: 2.7 million*
- *YouTube Subscribers: 584,000*
- **and counting!*

Not bad for a guy in his 70s.

What does this have to do with you, you're probably asking?

Imagine having an audience of people who like what you do and are connected to you. Not only do they buy your books, or shirts, listen to your music, and attend your concerts but they continue to do so long after the mainstream public has moved on to new and different artists.

If you're working to create a business that lasts for years, you may want to work on creating an audience like this for yourself.

"But I'm not Paul McCartney," you say. And it's true—but if you're entertaining your customer base or providing them with valuable information, they can number in the tens of thousands or more.

Think of what it would mean to have an audience who is loyal to you and willing to read your emails, or watch your videos, and buy your products—and they continue to do so year after year.

This is possible for all of us. It may be at a different level from Paul McCartney, but we can do it.

You can use strategies similar to Paul's.

Some of these strategies are:

- Having a website that tells the world what you're doing and where you're going
- Creating a subscription list and asking for people's emails and contact information

- Having a fan club that people actually pay money to be a part of
- Being present and active on social media
- Creating new content regularly for your fans to enjoy

None of these are beyond what any of us can do.

We may not have the social media teams and marketing/PR people that the celebrities do, but we can create similar systems and implement the same strategies that work time and time again.

Chapter Thirteen

What You Can Have

CAN I BE PAINFULLY HONEST WITH YOU?

Facebook advertising, as all types of advertising, has a cost. The difference between Facebook advertising and running an ad in the paper or on TV or the radio is that you can measure your results.

It's difficult to get hard numbers on how many people came from a particular ad on traditional media, but with Facebook, you can see how much activity an ad generated. This can be a curse or a blessing.

The other day I was talking with a client who was unhappy with the performance of their Facebook campaign.

I was happy with the ads we were running. According to the numbers the client was giving me, we were getting new people walking into their business for $25 each. I thought, *that's great—you are getting total strangers to come to your business and try you out for only $25!*

After all, if you buy an ad in the paper you can easily spend $1,000. To get a $25 cost per customer from the paper, you would need 40 new customers from this one ad. Most newspaper ads don't do that well, and TV and radio don't either.

However, the client was unhappy. The problem wasn't the ads, the results themselves, or even our efforts . . . it was unrealistic expectations.

I hadn't prepared her for the reality of Facebook marketing. She had been reading and hearing about fabulous success stories from people who were getting new customers for pennies. What they don't tell you in those stories is that the business has run many ads before that didn't work. It takes time, and money, to hit upon the message and offer that works.

Facebook isn't a magic money machine. It's not an ATM, you know those machines at the bank that spit out cash when you are withdrawing money from one of your accounts.

Then again . . . I was kidding a teller a few weeks ago and asking if she had one of those machines at her house. She informed me that they do run out of money and have to be refilled.

I was sorry to hear that. I liked the thought of a machine that spits out the amount of money I want, whenever I want it, on demand.

Well, with Facebook you also have to put money in to get money out. It can and does give you a great return on the time and money invested, but you do have an investment up front.

Depending on your business, $25 may seem high for a first-time customer. But it also may seem really cheap.

The point is that your advertising's job is to get people into your business, either online or to your physical store, and then it's your job to get them to come back. After all, it's easier to sell to a person who has already purchased one of your items than it is to sell someone who has never purchased anything from you.

Once you have your system working you'll be able to replicate it and step on the gas harder to get more customers, faster.

Set realistic expectations. Test and get an offer that works and an audience that responds to it, and then put the pedal to the metal to get fast results.

We've worked with clients in a variety of businesses. You've already seen some of their stories in this book's case studies, but let me tell you another story about how one long-time business added Facebook to their marketing and accelerated their growth, utilizing all of the elements we've discussed.

A classic success story

I met Steve Anderson, one of the owners of Workamper News, at a mastermind meeting. We were both members and we talked many times over meals and on breaks.

Workamper News is a community for RVers who travel in their RVs or want to travel full time in their RVs, who are also looking for ways to either reduce their expenses or who want to earn some extra income in a fun place doing a job they enjoy.

I could see what Steve had and the advantages of using Facebook to market his business, but as an experienced business owner, he didn't see the possibilities right away.

Here are the reasons why I was so sure that Facebook would work for them:

1. They had a large email list they communicated with regularly. (They jumped on the email marketing bandwagon in the mid-'90s.)

2. They had an active website that many of their members and people exploring the possibility of Workamping came to often. (Again, their first website was put up in the mid-'90s.)

3. They had an active Facebook page with over 15,000 Likes. The fans were engaged in posting, Liking, commenting, and sharing the posts from Workamper News, and they weren't doing much to make this happen.

4. They had a large library of articles and information that RVers found valuable.

5. They had a recognized name in their industry and they are well liked by their audience.

6. RVers are active on Facebook. After all, even though they are living their dreams, they want to keep up with family and friends all over the country, and Facebook is a great way to do that.

All of these items are assets that can be leveraged into success on Facebook. When you combine these assets with offers that your audience likes, you can really amp up your results.

After some consideration, Steve decided to "test" Facebook and see what might happen. We started by taking Workamper's email lists and uploading them to Facebook.

Steve had an email list of tens of thousands of people that we uploaded to Facebook. This let him reach these people in a different way. Yes, you can email them for free, but do you have 100 percent open rates in your emails?

When you combine Facebook ads with emails both delivering a similar message, you'll find that the response from both types of media will improve.

The next step we took was getting the Facebook pixel onto Workamper's website. Until you put the pixel on your site, Facebook doesn't start collecting data. Once you start collecting the data, you can target the visitors to your site with messages when you choose to.

Next, we moved to their Facebook fans and the friends of their fans. This group was very receptive to the messages we sent them. We told this group about any new events we were having or any new products we had, as well as offering people who weren't members the chance to become members.

We took advantage of Workamper's large library of articles by promoting information from their library to these different groups of people. This helped strengthen Workamper's great reputation within the community.

All of this ensures that Workamper's audience keeps growing and that they stay engaged. What has this enabled Workamper to do?

Workamper has been able to add over 30,000 new intro members in the past year. Since then, many of these people have taken the next steps to become full-fledged members.

Facebook has also enabled Workamper to sell their Training Triad course they created in combination with Terry Cooper from the Mobile RV Academy. This is a live five-day course that teaches the students how to fix 80 percent of the issues that they could have with their RVs.

This course sells for $1,644 and over the past several years we have helped sell hundreds of these courses using Facebook.

They have a recorded version of the class and they sell even more of these every month. These sell for $397 and offer a discount for the live course.

Workamper also uses Facebook to fill webinars for Workamper. When Workamper wants to talk about a new product or service, it is announced via Facebook and many signups are generated.

Workamper also uses their Facebook audiences to sell out their yearly gathering (Workamper Rendezvous), which is held each fall in Heber Springs, Arkansas. Once the event information is put together, they use Facebook to promote it to interested parties.

Workamper is using Facebook in many ways.

They are creating a steady stream of new customers who are being introduced to the idea of Workamping, and in many cases, they are enabling their members to live the life of their dreams much sooner than they anticipated.

Next, they are staying connected with their existing members, helping them to live the life they want a little more easily. This has helped Workamper retain their members for a longer period of time.

Along with staying longer, their members are also are more willing to buy from them. They sign up for events sooner, and they regularly purchase products from Workamper.

All of this has helped Workamper grow and thrive over the past few years. The combination of a great product and promoting it in many different ways (including Facebook) is a powerful combination.

Applying our Facebook strategies has been extremely effective for Workamper and the clients described in our other case studies. But did you ever hear the saying, "The cobbler's children have no shoes."?

Sometimes it's hard to see what's right in front of us.

When I think about how much this one oversight has cost me, it makes me sick to my stomach.

Let me tell you a personal story . . .

We own a laundromat in our hometown of Eau Claire, Wisconsin. We had a spare piece of land next to another business and we wanted to do something with this lot.

So we decided a laundromat would be just the ticket. And to be fair, it has worked out well over all the years we've owned it. But . . .

A few months back my sister and I were talking and she mentioned seeing another laundromat in our town advertising on Facebook and she wondered why we weren't.

That hit me hard. After all, I own a Facebook marketing company. Why wasn't I using Facebook to promote it?

After I thought about it for a bit, I remembered a talk we had with our accountant shortly after we opened the laundromat. He informed us that the location of the business and a nice sign on the building were all we would need. He had never seen a laundromat advertise effectively any other way.

We took his word and the business took off, grew a few years, and stabilized. I forgot about it. The laundromat just chugs along doing what it does within a few dollars every year.

The thing is that the conversation I mention here happened in the late '80s.

There are more options now than ever for promoting a business and many of them don't cost much money like, you know, Facebook.

I didn't even have to learn how to use Facebook or what strategy to use. In an hour we had a Facebook page set up and were running our first ad. Even for an expert, starting with nothing takes a little time.

The results we've gotten have astounded us and made us happy but as I look at how much money I could have made had I done this earlier . . . I get a little depressed, too.

Here is what we did. Since our market is in a fixed location and people visit it, we are limited by what audience we can target. But on the other hand, that also makes our job easier too.

So we targeted everyone living within five miles of the laundromat. Our goal, or objective, was to raise awareness that we existed. We have used both page post engagement ads and local awareness ads.

Our budget is $5 a day and we have the ads running four days a week. We have tested running the ads seven days a week, and the results are just as good with four days.

So now that we're spending money advertising, what do we get from it?

Since what we're selling can't be bought online I don't have the number of sales directly related to Facebook, but here is what happened with the sales:

The first six weeks our sales showed an increase of 20 percent over the past year. Since then we've leveled off with a consistent 10 percent increase and this is a business that has been stable for years.

We now spend about 15 minutes a week managing the Facebook account for this business and we're spending approximately $20 a week for a 10 percent increase in sales over a year.

We are getting more than a 10-to-1 return on our investment of money in Facebook.

Setting up and managing a campaign for a small local business isn't hard. It can be created and maintained with a small amount of time invested.

And better yet, there is nothing fancy needed. No custom audiences, or Pixels, or elaborate multi-step funnels with email autoresponder and multiple landing pages needed. With just an engaging ad to people around the business, we're seeing success.

If you have a local business, I would give this strategy a try. Who knows? Maybe you will be the one feeling a little sick to your stomach as you look at the increase in your sales, but feeling happy when you see your checkbook balance.

Can you use Facebook to market to businesses?

Chances are you've heard about Facebook marketing and then thought, "my customers are businesses," so you decided that you didn't want to give Facebook a try. This is what we at Go Social Experts do with Facebook to market our business, and yes, our customers are all business owners.

Since we are a Facebook marketing company we kind of have to use Facebook, and that is a good thing.

True confession time: When we get busy and are running behind, we put our Facebook work on hold to take care of our clients, so there are times when we have gaps in our own Facebook work.

We use Facebook in multiple ways. As you know there are three ways to grow your business.

1. Get more customers.
2. Get your customers to buy more.
3. Get your customers to come back more often.

We use Facebook for all of the these, just not at the same time.

For those of you who don't know what we do, these are the core services that we sell.

We offer an online training course (www.gosocialexperts.com/smartfacebookmarketing) for businesses who want to do everything themselves. This is great for those who have the time to study and work on their own, and who may be lacking the budget for our more expensive options.

Next, we offer a coaching program (www.gosocialexperts.com/done-with-you-facebook-funnel-creation/) for those who want to get results faster. It's like hiring a physical trainer to work out with you instead of reading articles and designing a workout program on your own. Once you're done with the program you'll have an entire Facebook marketing plan in place and running that has been tested and optimized. After completion, you— or the person you designated to do this—will know how to edit the marketing plan and how to create another system when you want to.

Finally, for or those that want someone to just do all the work for them, we offer a Done For You Service (www.gosocialexperts.com/done-for-you-facebook-funnel-creation/). You give us the information we need, and we implement all of it. This is for the company that knows what they want but don't have the time or staff to run Facebook campaigns profitably.

Get new customers

Let's start with our organic (unpaid) posting. We promote our blog posts to the people who have liked our Facebook page. We have gotten these likes both from organic work and from our paid work. Either way, as long as they're interested in your topic they are valuable to you.

We also talk about upcoming events, where we are, what we're doing, events we're attending, etc. All of this helps create a connection with our audience. They know that we're real people. By the way, this is the hardest for me. I tend to be a private person, and don't always think to share this information especially when I'm traveling.

On the paid side, we regularly are running ads to find new prospects for our services.

We start out by promoting our blog posts or videos to an audience who we think may find them valuable.

As you know, Facebook has incredible targeting options. I will mention two criteria we use. One, we put what we call income filters on our ads. We make sure that we're targeting people making over a certain amount of money. That way we know that they can afford our services. Second, we only target people who are Admins on a Facebook page. Both of these targeting strategies have helped us improve our Facebook ads results.

Once people look at a blog post or watch part of a video, we then offer them one of our lead magnets. We give them a reason to give us their name and/or email. One of our most popular lead magnets currently is our Facebook Live Tip Sheet, (www.gosocialexperts.com/FBLiveTips). All of this brings a steady flow of new people into our marketing system.

Get your existing customers to buy more

Once you've been in business for some time and have been generating income, you have existing customers. How can you use Facebook to get your existing customers to buy more?

To start with, we encourage all our customers to like us on Facebook. This gives us a way to stay connected. When they like us on Facebook, they will see some of the posts we put on Facebook. So, as long as we're solving problems for them or strengthening our relationships, we are building relationships with our existing customers. We also upload our email list to Facebook to create a custom audience.

We target our customer list with specific product offers. We talk to them about new services we're offering, as well as services they haven't purchased yet.

Staying connected in an unobtrusive way works. Our existing customers stay aware of us and many of them buy more of our products and services.

Get them to come back more often

We target our existing customer list for this too, the same as above. Here we're looking at how we get people to come back more often instead of how we get them to buy more.

When we have material that relates how others have been successful with our strategies, we'll make sure to run a small ad to our email list explaining that.

Many times that will bring up an "I never thought of that" and we'll get a call from a client either starting a service again or wanting to expand what they're already doing.

Either way, it's more income for us, and the clients get even better results, an all-around win.

Staying in contact with your existing customers is an affordable way to bring in a steady stream of new business.

All of the above has enabled Go Social Experts to grow consistently year after year. As I look back on what we did a few years ago and compare it to now, I'm amazed at how far we've come.

What I used to consider a "big win" would now be considered a marginal response that needs work. As you work on growing your audiences and communicating with them regularly through Facebook, you'll find that your results will start growing too.

Chapter Fourteen

Planning for Success

I HAVE SEEN IT far too often—a savvy, worthy businessperson misses out on an opportunity to grow their business and their profits. Why? Because they're too busy.

What does that mean, though? Who is too busy for something wonderful like opportunity, growth, and increased revenue?

Well, maybe YOU are. Do you . . .

- Feel like you can't do one more thing?
- Sometimes see the added work of opportunity and growth, rather than the benefits?
- Feel like you can't learn anything new because your head is too full of information already?
- Wish someone would just take something off your plate just so you can breathe?
- Avoid attending events because you don't have time or see the benefit—even if your ideal customers would be there too?
- Not want to try new things—especially when it comes to marketing. If it's worked in the past, why waste time on changing anything?

Or . . . maybe if one more person tells you how good Facebook is and that you should use it—or use it differently—you're going to pull your hair out (or if you're like me, what little hair you have left!).

I've been there too, my friends. Every entrepreneur has. We wouldn't have gotten this far if we didn't put our heads down and get stuff done—am I right?

There absolutely are times we need to put our heads down and get work done. But we also need to recognize the times when we need to lift our heads up, look around, and see what we can do to improve our results.

What happens when we keep our heads down too long?

- **Life becomes a grind.** We're getting up every day. We're working every day. But we never seem to get everything done. Have you ever noticed that no matter how much you do the list never seems to end?
- **We ignore the positive.** We end up getting so focused on the mountain of work before us, we miss the blue skies behind it.
- **Problem solving stops.** All we know is what we know and we stop looking for new possibilities. Maybe there are tools or different ways to do something that would alleviate some of the pressure but we're too blind to see them, much less seek them out.
- **Our relationships suffer.** Maybe you find yourself snapping at your employees or your family when you get home. You feel like if they could just see the heap of stress you're under, they'd understand and help you. But they don't, so you struggle alone.
- **We lose our energy.** Remember why you started this business or career in the first place? Do you still feel the same passion and energy as you once did?

And finally, when we close our minds to new opportunities we're putting ourselves in a perpetual cycle.

We keep putting forth the same effort and applying the same tactics and we keep finding ourselves in the same place. And then we continue to be frustrated by the place we're in.

Albert Einstein put it perfectly: "Insanity: doing the same thing over and over again and expecting different results."

Here's the thing, if you never try anything new (*Cough,

FACEBOOK, Cough*), if you don't meet new people and renew old relationships, if you don't open yourself up to new possibilities you're essentially expecting different results from the same activities.

And you'll find that you're not having as much fun.

When I find myself in this situation, I pick my head up and start looking around and I find that everything changes. I am energized by the possibility of new results when I create and implement new strategies. I find myself imagining a future that is different then what has been. I start dreaming about what I can do as my company grows.

How about you?

- *What do you want for your company in the next month, next year, or even in five years?*
- *Better yet, what are you doing to get there? (The same old thing?)*
- *Have you changed how you market?*
- *Have you changed who you are marketing to?*
- *Are you any more efficient in delivering your products then you were six months or a year ago so that you can grow and be able to fill the demand?*

Taken all at one time, these questions can feel overwhelming. But when you break them down, put them into a system, and start at the beginning you'll find yourself looking at your business and your life with new eyes.

As you complete the first step you'll be energized to move to the next step and then the next.

The most important thing I can suggest—from one businessperson to another—is to pick your head up, look around, and take a breath.

Find support

Have you noticed it's easier to help someone else with their business than it is to work on your own?

"It is literally true that you can succeed best and quickest by helping others to succeed." —Napoleon Hill

"Thousands of candles can be lighted from a single candle, and the life of the candle will not be shortened. Happiness never decreases by being shared." —Buddha

Let's face it, we've all been in this situation: we're working on a challenge, problem, or opportunity for our business, and we can't find a solution, but then we help other people with similar challenges in their business and we have several solutions for them.

Considering that I'm a marketing consultant whom people pay to help them, sometimes it can be embarrassing not to have the answer to a marketing question when it's related to my own business.

Why is it that I can find answers to others' challenges more easily than my own?

There have been times when I'm talking to the people who cut my hair and our conversation turns to their business. They are struggling with an issue and—to me—the answer seems simple. We talk it over and they try my suggestions. The next time I'm in for a haircut, they mention that my ideas worked well for them.

Sometimes I'm talking with a friend who mentions struggling with an issue. We talk it through, and, between the two of us, we come up with several possible solutions. My friend picks one, tries it, and has success.

I'm not sure why this happens, but I'm going to guess that it's a case of being too close to the forest to see the trees. In other words, when you're so close to the challenge, and so involved, you see limited options for a solution—or maybe no solution.

How do you overcome this and solve your challenges?

You have some options.

One solution is to find a confidant with whom to share your problem. You can get together or chat on the phone and as you explain your challenge, the two of you talk about solving the problem.

Another solution is to find or set up a group of people who get together weekly to help each other with their challenges. This suggestion is based on Napoleon Hill's Mastermind principle, in which a group of people gets together in agreement to come up with solutions that none of the individuals working alone would have even considered.

This approach does work. I participate in two of these groups. One is local and meets weekly, and the other is a regional group and meets by phone.

Both groups often help me with solutions I never would have considered otherwise.

Another idea is to write out your challenge as a question and give it to someone else to ask you. Then have them ask you the question and take notes of your answer. You'll be amazed at the answers you'll come up with.

These are some ideas you may not have considered. I've found all of the above solutions to be helpful; however, there are times when you need more help than the people you know can give you.

In these cases, you may want to consider hiring a professional. These people have many different titles; the most common of which are coach or consultant.

Coaches and consultants have a wide variety of skills. Make sure you pick one who has experience with your particular challenge.

If you're looking for help with Facebook advertising and how to use Facebook profitably, I have several options to choose from.

If you want help implementing a specific program, you can schedule a complimentary consultation call at www.gosocialexperts. com/free. We'll discuss your needs, and I'll help you develop your own Facebook marketing plan. If you want help implementing it, I can provide that, but if you want to do it on your own, that's fine too—I'll wish you well. I just ask that you let me know how well the plan worked so I can add you to my file of success stories.

You now have several options to help you move through your challenges, so you have no reason to stay stuck. The answer you're seeking is either tucked away in your own mind or waiting for you in someone else's.

Choose one of the tactics listed above and go out and find a solution so you can keep moving forward and achieving your goals.

Chapter Fifteen

Final Thoughts

I WAS TALKING with one of my mentors and whining a little. (Once in a while all of us have a weak moment.) This is what she said to me: "Complacency is a great place to visit, but a poor place to live."

I was complaining about the fact that I would have success and reach a goal, and then get stuck there for some time.

And that was frustrating me.

I had just reached a goal, but only a goal, not my big hairy audacious goal and I didn't want to leave and move on to the next goal. After all working for a goal you really want to achieve is hard. It means that I have to move outside my comfort zone. I must do things that aren't familiar, but the familiar is what has brought me the success I've had so far, and now I have something to lose.

It's easier to take risks when you have little to lose.

But then I think of where I want to be. I look at where I'm at versus where I want to be and I get past complacency and go back to work.

I know where I want to go and I'm determined to get there. I have people who care about me and want to see me reach my dreams, so they don't let me sit around complacent for long.

We all have times when we either feel like giving up because it's so hard, or we think, where I am now is pretty good, so why should I finish?

We all need people who keep us moving forward towards our dreams. Finding these one or two people who make sure you keep moving is one of the keys to success.

What keeps you moving forward? When you're looking at implementing Facebook marketing and it's not working the way you wanted it to, what keeps you trying one more time?

When your Facebook campaigns are working pretty good, and you're getting decent results, what keeps you coming back to get even better results?

And when you're crushing it, every campaign is returning big numbers for you, why do you try something new? As an aside here, you don't stop what's working, you add new campaigns. Never stop something profitable that works for something untested.

For those who will keep experimenting and trying new things there are rewards. What gets you up and keeps you moving?

Those of us who keep experimenting and trying new things will find success in all the endeavors we undertake.

Keep experimenting, testing, and implementing and you'll be one of the people having great success with your Facebook marketing. Your friends and competitors will be wondering what you're doing and how you're generating such success.

You can smile and know that you put in the work, learned the skills, and implemented what you learned so that you could reach this level.

Congratulations on reaching this part of the book. If you're like me, you might have skipped here without reading the entire book first. Welcome.

I've put together a FREE masterclass on Facebook marketing. It will show you what it takes to get up and running online and what you need to consider to profit from your Facebook marketing. You can sign up for it at www.gosocialexperts.com/masterclass.

Here are some other ways to stay connected with me:

I publish blog posts regularly at www.gosocialexperts.com/blog. You can keep up with all my latest discoveries and teachings there.

I concentrate on Facebook marketing, but you'll find other topics related to running your business and improving your life there too.

You can follow me on Facebook at Facebook.com/GoSocialExperts

on Twitter at https://twitter.com/GoSocialExperts

on Instagram at https://www.instagram.com/go.social/ and

on LinkedIn at http://www.linkedin.com/in/brianthahn

And if you're ready to accelerate your Facebook marketing schedule a complimentary Facebook call with me. We'll talk see what you want to accomplish and decide if we're a good fit for each other. To schedule your call go to www.gosocialexperts.com/callbrian30.

And no matter when you're reading this: Have a great day!

About the Author

BRIAN HAHN is the Founder/CEO of Go Social Experts. He specializes in helping business owners and their teams profitably use Facebook and Online Marketing. He takes an innovative approach to Facebook marketing based on his knowledge of Facebook and his 30+ years of owning businesses in the various industries to custom build a system just for you. He's the author of two other books as well as the creator of "The Ultimate Facebook Marketing System" which teaches business owners and their team  how to profitably use Facebook for marketing their business. Over the past seven years, Brian has worked with over 300 businesses in the United States and Canada to develop and implement Facebook marketing systems. He supports Special Olympics and The Children's Miracle Network as well as the Boy Scouts of America where he was a registered leader for over 14 years.

www.ExpertPress.net